previous page **David Bowie,**
whose feminine clothing and
make-up helped publicize
his music

below **The Beatles,** whose
haircuts in 1963 caused even more
comment than David Bowie's
bi-sexual image in the 1970s.
clockwise from left:
George Harrison
Paul McCartney
Ringo Starr
John Lennon

GREAT POP STARS

Andy Gray

Managing Editor, 'New Musical Express'

Hamlyn
London
New York
Sydney
Toronto

Published by
The Hamlyn Publishing Group Limited
London   New York   Sydney   Toronto
Astronaut House, Feltham, Middlesex,
England

© The Hamlyn Publishing Group Limited, 1973

ISBN 0 600 38696 1

Printed in Great Britain
by Hazell Watson & Viney Limited,
Aylesbury, Bucks

Acknowledgments

The publishers are grateful to the following for the
illustrations reproduced in this book:

Associated British Pictures Corporation
Atlantic Records
Barratt's Photo Press
Camera Press
Capitol Records Inc.
Columbia Records
Decca Records
Robert Ellis
Epoque Ltd.
Focus Press
Andrew Gray
Dezo Hoffmann
IPC Magazines
Keystone Press Agency
New Musical Express
Nevins-Kirshner Assoc.
Paul Popper
Pictorial Press
RCA Records
David Redfern
Ron Reid
Richard Gersh Assoc.
SKR Photos
Syndication International
Thames Television
United Artists Corporation
Universal Pictorial Press
Warner Bros. Records Inc.

CONTENTS

INTRODUCTION

Elvis Presley, as he is best remembered by pop fans

In writing about the most successful recording artists and their records of the pop era, from 1955 to the present day, I have had a very difficult task in choosing who to include and who to exclude. To name everyone who has made records over the nineteen year period would require a volume much bigger than this one. So I have chosen those who have won Gold Record Awards for sales of a million copies or who have topped either the American or British charts, or whose discs have sold consistently well over a long period.

Almost every year record sales increase and we have seen American domination and then British leadership in international disc tastes, until now, in the '70s, it seems to have reached a 50—50 level, and what sells well in America also sells well in Britain and in the other pop countries. Sales in America are vastly greater than in Britain or elsewhere and many American artists can sell a million within their own country, while few British stars can sell a million within Britain alone.

When one considers the enormous output of the ever-increasing number of recording companies, one realises that the task of naming the most successful discs of each year is not simple, and I would not expect my judgment to satisfy everybody. We all have our favourites and I apologise in advance for any omissions. As Editor of the "New Musical Express", one of the world's most successful music weekly papers, for 15 years, I have lived with the recording industry through the years I am writing about and ought, at least, to know it pretty well.

In all cases I have tried to mention a disc within the year it was made, and not the year it qualified for a Gold Record. Some sold quickly and earned their awards within 12 months, but some sold over a longer period. Some records mentioned may have been on sale in different countries at different times, and I have always mentioned the year they were first on sale.

The research I have put into compiling the text of this pictorial book has been a pleasure to me and I hope it will jog memories and bring back thoughts of stars and songs which have brought us much happiness in the past.

My thanks for assistance from the charts of the "New Musical Express" and "Cash Box", the awards of the RIAA, and Joseph Murrells' "Daily Mail Book of Golden Discs".

ANDY GRAY
April, 1973

1955

This year saw the beginning of the great transformation from rather urban singers and bands to the wilder aspects of a rhythm-and-blues that had been in America for a long time but was about to achieve world acclaim for the first time, under the name of rock'n'roll.

It was also the year the gramophone, with its one-speed of 78 revolutions per minute and its heavy, breakable 78 records, was to be replaced by the record player, with a three and four speed turntable, playing not only the old 78s, but the brand new 45 rpm singles, 33 rpm long-playing records, and 16 rpm talking books and other spoken word discs. The 45s, 33s and 16s were pressed onto much thinner, lighter, unbreakable discs, with mini-grooves that could contain a lot more music in a smaller space, played by more sensitive playing arms with a "needle" known as a stylus, using diamonds and sapphires.

In 1954 an exuberant Detroit-born guitarist-singer called **Bill Haley**, with a wild group called the **Comets**, had struck it rich with a new, crazy kind of beat music that made you want to dance, and a piece called *Shake, Rattle And Roll*, which made the world do just that! Bill followed it up with *Rock Around The Clock*, another earth-shattering multi-million seller. Both tunes still sell today and in 1955 confirmed the fact that rock'n'roll was here to stay.

Aiding and abetting Haley were **Chuck Berry's** *Maybelline*, **LaVerne Baker's** *Tweedle Dee*, **Pat Boone's** *Ain't That A Shame*, **Fats Domino's** *Thinking of You*, *All By Myself*, *I Can't Go On* and *Ain't That A Shame*; **Little Richard's** *Tutti Frutti* and **The Platters'** *Only You*. All these records came out in America during 1955 and were known world-wide within a year or so.

Of course, rock didn't have it all its own way. **Frank Sinatra**, long a million-seller by 1955, continued to keep his fans happy with *Young At Heart*, *Love And Marriage*, *Tender Trap* and *Learnin' The Blues*. **Perry Como** maintained his popularity with *Ko Ko Mo* and *Tina Maria*, and **Tennessee Ernie** (Ford) had the record named the best seller in Britain in 1955, *Give Me Your Word*, with another country singer, **Slim Whitman**, second with *Rose Marie*. **Tony Bennett**, **Guy Mitchell**, **Sammy Davis Jr.**, **Dean Martin** and **Nat King Cole** were other American singers with world following.

Dean's big hit of 1955 was *Memories Are Made of This*, which in Britain was successfully covered by **Dave King** later. Another very popular song of the year was *Stranger in Paradise*, with four versions doing well, by **The Four Aces**, **Tony Bennett**, **Tony Martin** and trumpeter **Eddie Calvert**, of *Oh Mein Papa* fame. And **Billy Hayes** had plenty of opposition with *The Ballad Of Davy Crockett*, but won the Gold Disc for it.

The instrumental hit of the year was pianist **Roger Williams'** *Autumn Leaves*, while **Billy Vaughn** and his Orchestra won fame with *Melody Of Love*, the French tune which sold over a period of four years. **Mitch Miller**, with his orchestra and chorus, had a massive hit with *Yellow Rose of Texas*, and **Art Mooney's** Orchestra sold a million with *Honey Babe*. **Les Baxter** did the same with *Unchained Melody*.

Another smash hit orchestral number which captured the world's ears was *Cherry Pink And Apple Blossom White* by Mambo King **Perez Prado** and his Orchestra, with **Billy Regis** playing trumpet. In Britain, **Eddie Calvert** shared the hit with Prado. And **Winifred Atwell** won two Gold Records for her piano Party discs.

Ted Heath and **Mantovani** were the leaders in their fields, both enjoying world fame. Ted's vocalists, **Lita Roza** and **Dickie Valentine**, launched out on their own and had immediate success, particularly Dickie with two of the year's big hits, *Finger of Suspicion* and *Christmas Alphabet*.

Another hit singer was our present-day British deejay, **Jimmy Young**, who had two No. 1 hits with *Unchained Melody* and *Man From Laramie*. **David Whitfield** was another constant chart-maker following his *Cara Mia* world hit.

Two of America's most dynamic singers — **Johnnie Ray** and **Frankie Laine** — had a good year, Johnnie following up his famous *Cry* and *Little White Cloud That Cried* with his 1955 hits — *Hernando's Hideaway*, *Hey There* and *Song Of The Dreamer*, while Frankie, of *Mule Train* and *Jezebel* fame, had a big seller with *Cool Water*.

Among the ladies, **Rosemary Clooney**, **Peggy Lee** and **Ella Fitzgerald** were most popular world-wide, and in America **Julie London** (*Cry Me A River*), the **McGuire Sisters** (*Sincerely*), **Jo Stafford** (*Make Love To Me*), **Georgia Gibbs** (*Tweedle Dee*, *Dance With Me Henry*), **Gogi Grant** (*Suddenly There's A Valley*), **Gale Storm** (*I Hear You Knocking*), **Joni James** (*How Important Can It*

Tony Bennett, a popular singer all over the world

1
Ruby Murray

2
Perry Como

3
Pat Boone

4
Bill Haley and The Comets

Be), and **The Chordettes** girl group *(Mr Sandman)*.

In Britain we had our own female stars, including **Vera Lynn**, who had won over America previously with *Auf Wiederseh'n Sweetheart*, **Ruby Murray**, whose *Softly Softly* and *Evermore* were the big hits of the year and who had the distinction of having five records simultaneously in the Top Twenty during 1955*, and the late **Alma Cogan** with *Dreamboat*. **Rosemary Clooney's** *Mambo Italiano* was another major seller in Britain during 1955.

Indeed, a survey of 1955 based on the "New Musical Express" chart entries for the year put **Ruby Murray** way ahead in the British chart section, with **Jimmy Young** second and **Frankie Laine** third. And in the American charts, another girl singer, **Georgia Gibbs**, came first, with **Perez Prado** and **Bill Haley** second and third, their records *Cherry Pink* and *Rock Around The Clock* coming first and second in the American top selling record section.

* A feat equalled by Bill Haley in 1956 and Elvis Presley in 1957.

1

2

3

4

5

1
Frankie Laine

2
Vera Lynn

3
Johnnie Ray

4
Rosemary Clooney

5
Guy Mitchell

6
Ella Fitzgerald

1956

If 1955 was the *hors-d'oeuvre* of the pop era, 1956 was certainly the meat course. It heralded one of the two great phenomena of the musical times — **Elvis Presley** (the other was **The Beatles**). Born in 1935 in the southern state of Mississippi, **Presley's** natural talent for singing with equal ease a rhythm-and-blues or a country-and-western, or a ballad song has kept him at the top ever since, and the fact that he is now 38 means nothing to his millions of fans.

Presley's statistics make the mind boggle and keep a corps of auditors busy. The first of his over 260 million-selling records over 17 years happened with *Heartbreak Hotel/I Was The One*, after he had paid to make a record at the age of 19 as a birthday present for his mother. The recording manager at the Sun studios in Memphis asked him to record some more and paid a nominal fee to him. Later his contract was bought by RCA for only 35,000 dollars.

His hip-swinging stage exuberance and his clean-cut American-boy good-looks made him an instant teenagers' hero, after he had been seen nationwide on Ed Sullivan's TV show and in the film "Love Me Tender". His *Heartbreak Hotel* appeared in the U.S. charts in March and soon was top.

His emergence was slower in Britain. The first trade paper advertisement appeared on March 30, quoting a review by the "Daily Mirror" pop man Pat Doncaster, who wrote: "Take a dash of **Johnnie Ray**, add a sprinkling of **Billy Daniels** and what have you got — **Elvis Presley**." He was bannered as "King Of The Western Bop.'. But it wasn't until May that the record got in the charts and then made slow progress, reaching No. 2 but never getting to the top.

In America, however, he was soon No. 1 and surrounded by many other rock'n'roll records by **Bill Haley** *(See You Later Alligator, Rockin' Thru The Rye, Rip It Up)*, **Carl Perkins** *(Blue Suede Shoes)*, **The Teen-Agers** with **Frankie Lyman** *(Why Do Fools Fall In Love?)*, **The Platters** *(Great Pretender, My Prayer)*, 16-million seller **Fats Domino** *(Bo Weevil, I'm In Love Again, Blueberry Hill* and *Blue Monday)*, **Bill Doggett** *(Honky Tonk Parts 1 and 2)*, **Little Richard** *(Long Tall Sally, Rip It Up)*, **Chuck Berry** *(Roll Over Beethoven)*, **James Brown and the Famous Flames** *(Please, Please, Please)* and **Gene Vincent and the Blue Caps** *(Be-Bop-A-Lulu, Bluejean Bop)*.

But **Elvis** was the leader and he added during 1956 three other million sellers to *Heartbreak Hotel* — *I Want You, I Need You, I Love You, Hound Dog/Don't Be Cruel*, and *Love Me Tender/Any Way You Want Me*.

On the fringe of rock was the swinger **Pat Boone**, still adding to his million-sellers with *I'll Be Home, I Almost Lost My Mind, Friendly Persuasion, Remember You're Mine*, plus near millions with *Long Tall Sally* and *Tutti Frutti*. **Little Willie John** won a Gold Disc for his more soulful rhythm-and-blues version of *Fever* (two years before **Peggy Lee's** disc), and **Johnnie Ray** scored another million with *Just Walkin' In The Rain*.

Lonnie Donegan's *Rock Island Line* proved popular in America as well as Britain, where it started the do-it-yourself skiffle music craze which gave us so many of our music stars in later years. **Donegan** even had an LP and an EP selling as many copies as singles in those days, and among his hits were *Lonnie Donegan Showcase, Skiffle Session, Stewball, Lost John* and *Bring A Little Water Sylvie*.

The **Dream Weavers** had an international hit with *It's Almost Tomorrow*, while in Britain **Ronnie Hilton** topped with *No Other Love*, **Max Bygraves** invited you to *Meet Me On the Corner*, **Frank Sinatra** had *The Tender Trap*, **Mel Torme** sang of *Mountain Greenery*, **Ruby Murray** told us *You Are My First Love*, and **Anne Shelton** asked us to *Lay Down Your Arms*. Other British chart hits were **Malcolm Vaughan's** *St. Teresa Of The Roses*, **Mitch Miller's** *Song For A Summer Night*, **Freddie Bell and the Bell Boys'** *Giddy Up A Ding Dong*, **Andy Williams'** *Canadian Sunset*, **Frankie Laine's** *Woman In Love*, and **Guy Mitchell's** *Singing The Blues*, which was No. 1 in both America and Britain.

Three Americans versus Britons chart-honour battles occurred — **Jim Lowe** had the *Green Door* hit in America while **Frankie Vaughan** won it in Britain; **Les Baxter's Orchestra** sold a million with *Poor People Of Paris* in the USA, but pianist **Winifred Atwell** got the No. 1 in UK; and while **Jimmy Young's** *More* got to No. 1 in Britain, **Perry Como's** version sold a million in America, as did his *Hot Diggity*.

Country-and-western songs did well, specially **Tennessee Ernie's** *16 Tons*, **Kay Starr's** *Rock'n'Roll Waltz*, **Johnny Cash's** *I Walk The Line*, **Marvin Rainwater's** *Gonna Find Me A Blue Bird*, **George**

Elvis Presley came to the fore in 1956

ELVIS PRESLEY has been
'The King' of the
pop singers since 1956

1
Bing Crosby, Grace Kelly and Frank Sinatra, in the film "High Society"

2
Gene Vincent

3
Vic Damone, with Pier Angeli

4
Frankie Vaughan

19

1
Johnny Cash

2
Andy Williams

3
Johnny Mathis

1957

Rock'n'roll continued to flourish, with the King, **Elvis Presley** continuing to add million-selling hits — *Too Much/Playin' For Keeps, All Shook Up/That's When The Heartaches Begin, Loving You/Teddy Bear, Jailhouse Rock/Treat Me Nice*, and a "Rock'n'Roll" LP.

Four major newcomers to the rock scene had their first "million" hits during the year. **Buddy Holly**, who was killed in an air crash in 1959, won fame with his *Peggy Sue*, backed by the **Crickets**, who had a hit of their own, *That'll Be The Day*, with Buddy as a member of the group. The **Crickets** are still popular today.

So are the **Everly Brothers** — Don and Phil from Nashville and theatrical parents — whose first hits were *Bye Bye Love* and *Wake Up Little Susie*. **Jerry Lee Lewis** started the fashion, with **Little Richard**, of hammering the piano standing up as he let rip with his ravin', rockin' vocal style. He came from the Presley Sun Record school and struck Gold with *Whole Lotta Shakin' Goin' On* and *Great Balls Of Fire*. He still is a top-liner.

Ricky Nelson was the **David Cassidy** of 1956, winning fame first in his family's TV show and recording, aged 17, three million-sellers in the year — *A Teenager's Romance/I'm Walkin', Be-Bop Baby*, and *Stood Up/Waiting In School*.

Other r'n'r acts arrived on the scene during the year — **The Coasters** with *Searchin'/Young Blood*; **Danny And The Juniors**: *At The Hop*; **The Diamonds**: *Little Darlin'*; **Ivory Joe Hunter**: *Since I Met You Baby*; **Bill Justis Orchestra**: *Raunchy*; **Buddy Knox**: *Party Doll*; **Charlie Gracie**, and **Andy Williams**: both with *Butterfly*; **Del Vikings**: *Come Go With Me*; **Sal Mineo**: *Start Movin'*; **Tommy Sands**: *Teen Age Crush*; **Larry Williams**: *Short Fat Fanny*, and *Bony Maronie*; and piano-man **Huey Smith**: *Rockin' Pneumonia And The Boogie Woogie Flu*.

Old favourites consolidated earlier hits — **Chuck Berry** with *School Days*, and *Rock'n'Roll Music*; **Fats Domino** with *I'm Walkin', It's You I Love*, and *I Still Love You*; **Little Richard** with *Lucille, Jenny Jenny*, and *Keep A'Knockin'*; and **Gene Vincent** with *Wear My Ring*.

Even younger than **Ricky Nelson** was newcomer **Paul Anka**, a 14-year-old Canadian boy who wrote and recorded *Diana*, which sold millions round the world and made him a millionaire at 15. Today Paul is still a top entertainer and song writer. Another important newcomer, still a star today, was **Tommy Steele**, the personality of the year in Britain, and topping the charts with *Singing The Blues*, also a hit for **Guy Mitchell**. Two other newcomers — **Tab Hunter** and **Sonny James** — shared the same song as their hit, *Young Love*. The late **Sam Cooke** emerged with *You Send Me*, and *I'll Come Running Back To You*, while the **Four Preps** did well with *26 Miles*.

Pat Boone continued his meteoric career with four more million-selling, world-wide hits — *Love Letters In The Sand, Don't Forbid Me, Why Baby Why*, and *April Love/When The Swallows Come Back To Capistrano*. **Perry Como**, too, added a Gold Disc with *Round and Round*, and **Frank Sinatra** with *All The Way/Chicago*. **Johnny Mathis** had two more — *Chances Are* and *It's Not For Me To Say*, and **Frankie Laine** gave us *Moonlight Gambler*.

On the country-and-western front, **Marvin Rainwater** had another success, duetting *Majesty Of Love* with a young Italian-American lady who was destined for a major career, **Connie Francis**, and the late **Jim Reeves** introduced a record still popular today, *Four Walls*. **Marty Robbins** made it big with a jaunty tune, *A White Sports Coat And A Pink Carnation*, which brought the three **King Brothers** to fame in Britain. **Jimmie Rodgers** got his first Gold from *Honeycomb*.

Indication that the skiffle craze was at its height in Britain and spilling over into America was the international success of **Nancy Whiskey**, backed by **Chas. McDevitt's Skiffle Group**, of *Freight Train*. **Lonnie Donegan** continued to lead the field with two consecutive No. 1s in Britain with *Cumberland Gap*, and *Puttin' On The Style/Gamblin' Man*. Other skiffle personalities were **Johnny Duncan and his Blue Grass Boys**, **Shirley Douglas**, **The Vipers**, **Bob Cort** and **Sonny Stewart**.

Calypso, too, gained popularity via **Harry Belafonte**, who won Gold Records for his *B. Sings Of The Caribbean* LP, and singles of *Banana Boat Song, Mama Looka Boo Boo*, and the big Christmas song of 1957, *Mary's Boy Child*.

A remarkable 1957 artist was former Butlin Holiday Camp Redcoat **Russ Hamilton**, whose *We Will Make Love* got to No. 1 in Britain at the same time as the record's flip-side, *Rainbow*, became No. 1 in America. Russ wrote both sides. Another memorable disc was **Billy Williams'** version of *I'm Gonna Sit Right Down And Write Myself A Letter*.

Buddy Holly's short career at the top started in 1957

On the orchestral front, **Mantovani's** *Film Encores* LP, **Mitch Miller's** March from "Bridge On The River Kwai", **David Rose** with *Calypso Melody*, **Billy Vaughn** with *Sail Along Silv'ry Moon*, and **Jimmy Dorsey's** *So Rare* all won Golds.

Girl singers had a lean year, with only **LaVerne Baker** *(Jim Dandy)*, **Ruth Brown** *(Lucky Lips* — a Cliff Richard hit much later), and **Debbie Reynolds** *(Tammy)* winning Golds, although **Peggy Lee**, **Shirley Bassey**, veteran **Gracie Fields** and **Petula Clark** had hits in Britain during the year.

Frankie Vaughan did well with *Garden Of Eden* and *Wandering Eyes*, and **Johnnie Ray** got everyone swinging with *Not Tonight Josephine*, while **Jim Dale**, now in the "Carry On . . ." film team, had a big hit with *Be My Girl*.

But 1957 was definitely a year for the rockers.

1
Jim Dale

2
Tommy Steele

3
Shirley Bassey

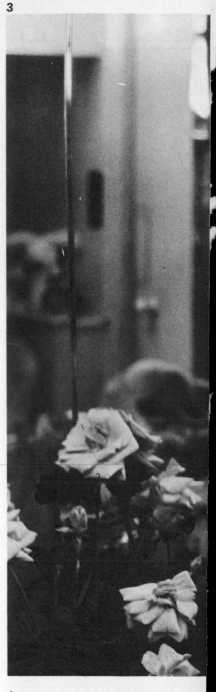

4
Eddie Fisher and Debbie Reynolds

5
Charles McDevitt, with Shirley Douglas

5

1

2

3

1
Sal Mineo

2
Paul Anka

3
Fats Domino

4
The Coasters

5
Chuck Berry

4

1958

This year was remarkable for the number of memorable songs we heard. While rock'n'roll beat tunes were still doing very well, there seemed to be a return to melody, with such songs, still remembered today, as *Catch A Falling Star/Magic Moments*, which gave **Perry Como** a very big hit, with **Ronnie Hilton** doing well in Britain, too, with *Magic Moments*; *All I Have To Do Is Dream* by the **Everly Brothers**; *It's All In The Game* by **Tommy Edwards**; *The Story Of My Life* by the late **Michael Holliday**; *Volare* by **Dean Martin** and the Italian composer **Domenico Modugno** (and comedian **Charlie Drake**); *Who's Sorry Now* by **Connie Francis**; and *It's Only Make Believe* by **Conway Twitty**.

Country-and-western made a strong melodic challenge, helped by **Don Gibson's** *Oh Lonesome Me*, **Billy Grammar's** *Gotta Travel On*, **George Hamilton IV's** *Why Don't They Understand?*; **Ray Price's** *City Lights*, **Jimmie Rodger's** *Secretly*, and **Marvin Rainwater's** *Whole Lotta Woman*.

Girl singers, too, made a comeback, led by **Connie Francis**, only 19, who had hits with *Who's Sorry Now, I'm Sorry I Made You Cry, Stupid Cupid, I'll Get By*, and *Fallin'*. **Peggy Lee** had a big one with *Fever*, and the **Chordettes** vocal group with *Lollipop* (a big hit for the British **Mudlarks** group, too). The **McGuire Sisters** had a *Sugartime* hit in America which **Alma Cogan** enjoyed in Britain, and **Petula Clark** had two hits, *Alone*, and *Baby Lover*. **Jane Morgan** sang well on *The Day The Rains Came* to make it a hit, and **Marion Ryan** did the same with *Love Me Forever*.

There were novelty hits from **David Seville**, using distorted sound for *Witch Doctor* and the *Chipmunk Song*, and **Sheb Wooley** with *Purple People Eater*. Cha-cha was popular and **Perez Prado's** *Patricia* and **Tommy Dorsey's** *Tea For Two Cha-Cha* sold over a million each. **Mantovani's** *Gems Forever* LP and **Billy Vaughn's** *La Paloma* were also in favour, as was pianist **Roger Williams'** *Till*.

Rhythm-and-blues record of the year was *What Am I Living For* by **Chuck Willis**, and folk-skiffle from America came from the **Kingston Trio's** *Tom Dooley*, which was also one of **Lonnie Donegan's** several hits of 1958. **Mitch Miller** made sing-along music popular and dynamic trumpeter-vocalist **Louis Prima**, with vocalist wife **Keely Smith**, livened things up with *That Old Black Magic*, and *Buona Sera*. **Louis** still is a favourite in Las Vegas.

But it was still the big beat boys who came out best. **Elvis Presley** kept up his amazing pace, despite the fact that he had been recruited into the U.S. Army during the year and shipped to Germany for foreign service. *Wear My Ring, Don't, Hard Headed Woman, Don't Ask Me Why* and *I Got Stung* were just five of his hits, while **Ricky Nelson** made more fans with *Poor Little Fool, Lonesome Town*, and *Believe In What You Say*.

Pat Boone had a swinging hit with *Wonderful Time Up There*, a gospel song, plus *Cherie I Love You* and *It's Too Soon To Know*, and **Chuck Berry** added *Sweet Little 16*, and *Johnny B. Goode*. The **Everlys** gave us *Bird Dog* and the **Coasters** *Yakkety Yak*.

The **Champs** pounded out *Tequila*, and **Danny And The Juniors** rocked *At The Hop*. The **Kalin Twins** made it with *When* and the **Platters** with *Twilight Time* and *Smoke Gets In Your Eyes*, an oldie.

Two notable newcomers were **Duane Eddy**, the 'twang' guitar man, with *Rebel Rouser*, and singer **Bobby Darin** with *Splish Splash* (**Charlie Drake** was his unlikely chart rival on this), and *Queen Of The Hop*. The late **Big Bopper** added *Chantilly Lace* and the cute **Poni Tails** girl group sang *Born Too Late*.

England's little **Laurie London**, aged 13, got to the top of the American charts with *He's Got The Whole World In His Hands* and sold a million, and a young Scots boy, **Jackie Dennis**, had a big hit with *La De Dah*. Even younger was **Dodie Stevens**, aged 11, an American kid who won a Gold with *Pink Shoelaces*.

As if these weren't enough beat hits, we also had: the late **Ritchie Valens**: *Donna/La Bamba*; **Little Anthony and The Imperials**: *Tears On My Pillow*; **Little Richard**: *Good Golly Miss Molly*; **Little Willie John**: *Talk To Me*; **Jerry Lee Lewis**: *Breathless*; **Clyde McPhatter**: *A Lover's Questions*; **James Brown**: *Try It (I Need You)*; **Jimmy Clanton**: *Just A Dream*, and *A Letter To An Angel*; **Bobby Helms**: *Jingle Bell Rock*; and **Buddy Holly**: *It Doesn't Matter Any More*.

In Britain, **Frankie Vaughan** was having a very big year with *Gotta Have Something In The Bank Frank* (with the **Kaye Sisters**), *Kisses Sweeter Than Wine, Can't Get Along Without You, Kewpie Doll* (winning a chart-race with **Perry Como** on this one), *Am I Wasting My Time*, and *Wonderful Things*, all in the best sellers.

Duane Eddy had a big hit in 1958 with *Rebel Rouser*

1
Dean Martin

2
Alma Cogan

3
Bobby Darin

A novel sound got to No. 1 – **Elias and the Zig Zag Jive Flutes** (of Johannesburg) playing *Tom Hark*. **Marty Wilde** had a big one with *Endless Sleep*, and **Max Bygraves** stayed in the charts a long time with *Tulips From Amsterdam/You Need Hands*. **Tommy Steele** had success with *Nairobi*, and Canadian **Tommy Scott** with *My True Love*. **Frankie Avalon** made it with *Gingerbread* and **Eddie Cochran** with *Summertime Blues*.

Finally, a newcomer who did very nicely with *Move It/High Class Baby*, his first record which got to No. 2, and who was voted Most Promising Singer of 1958 – **Cliff Richard**.

1

2

3

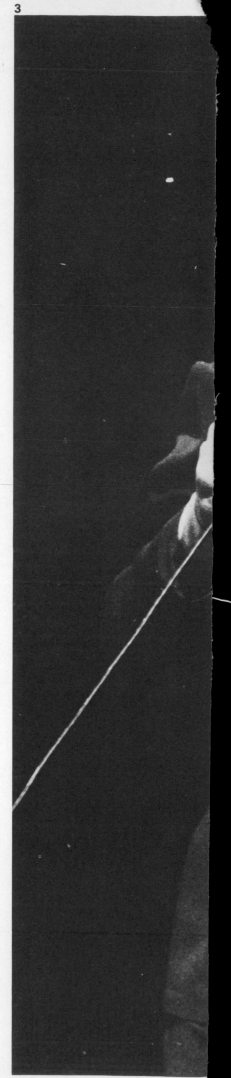

1
**Michael Holliday (left) with
The Allisons**

2
Peggy Lee

3
Connie Francis

1

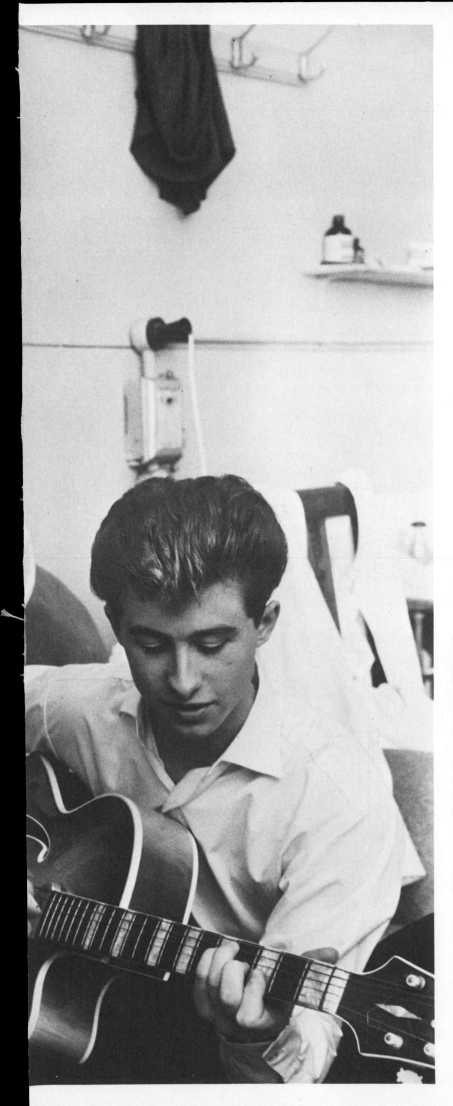

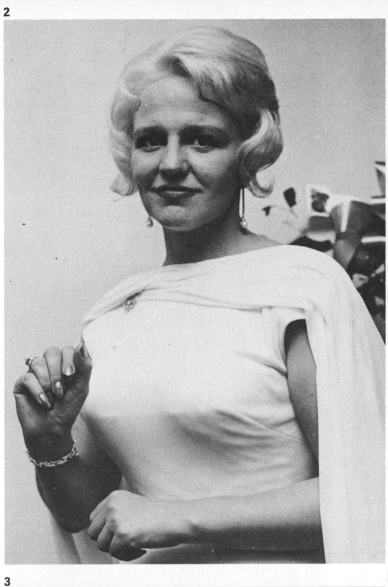

THE **B**EATLES won over
the entire world to
British pop music
after their breakthrough
in 1963

CILLA BLACK became the
first Merseybeat girl
singer in 1963 with
Love Of The World

1
Marion Ryan

2
Max Bygraves

3
Marty Wilde

1959

Changes were in the air during the year. Groups started to appear. Instrumental records were big sellers. Old time tunes were given beat treatment. And a whole batch of British newcomers arrived on the scene.

Among the groups to make their bow with Gold Records were **Dion and the Belmonts** with *Teenager In Love*; the **Browns** and **Les Compagnons de la Chanson**, both with *Three Bells* (about little Jimmy Brown), **The Fleetwoods** with *Come Softly To Me*; the **Isley Brothers** with *Shout* (a hit later for **Lulu**). **The Drifters** (American, and not **Cliff Richard's** group later named **The Shadows**) with *There Goes My Baby*; the **Impalas** with *Sorry*; **Emile Ford and the Checkmates** with *What Do You Want To Make Those Eyes At Me For?* and the **Avons** with *Seven Little Girls*.

Instrumental singles became popular, specially in Britain where **Russ Conway** occupied the No. 1 spot in the charts for several weeks with *Side Saddle* and then *Roulette*, both written by him. He also had *China Tea*, *More and More Party Pops*, *The World Outside* and *Snow Coach* in the best sellers during the year.

Trad bandleader-trombonist **Chris Barber and his Jazz Band** with **Monty Sunshine** on clarinet, won a Gold Disc for *Petite Fleur*, a top seller in America and Britain. Guitarist **Duane Eddy** sold many copies of *Peter Gunn*, *Yep* and *40 Miles of Bad Road* during the year, and guitarists **Santo and Johnny** won a Gold Disc for *Sleep Walk*. Other instrumental Golds went to drummer **Sandy Nelson** for *Teen Beat*; **Johnny and the Hurricanes** for *Red River Rock*, and the **Bill Black Combo** with *Smokie*. In France, **Frank Pourcel and the Rockin' Strings** won a Gold for a beaty *Only You*, and in Britain Top Ten recordings were **Lord Rockingham XI's** *Hoot Mon*, and *Wee Tom*; **Bert Weedon's** *Guitar Boogie Shuffle*, and **Winifred Atwell's** *Piano Party*.

The rock fans were demanding so many records some artists gave oldies a new beat treatment. **Connie Francis** led this with her massive hit, *Who's Sorry Now*, and followed it with an old **Ink Spots** number, *You Always Hurt The One You Love*. **Little Richard** revived *Baby Face*, a Jolson tune, and *By The Light Of The Silvery Moon*. **Fats Domino** gave Eddie Cantor's 1920 hit, *Margie*, new life, and **Conway Twitty** put beat into **Nat King Cole's** *Mona Lisa*, and Ireland's traditional *Danny Boy*! **The Platters** with *Smoke Gets In Your Eyes*, and **Paul Anka** with *My Heart Sings* were two more beat-infused revivals.

And in Britain, new life was put into the record industry by new artists, headed by **Cliff Richard**, a good-looking, pleasant, enthusiastic young singer, who had a very good year with a million-seller, *Living Doll*, written by Lionel Bart. He also had hits with *Livin' Lovin' Doll*, *Mean Streak*, *Travellin' Light* (a No. 1) and *Dynamite*.

Other British beat names to emerge were **Adam Faith** (No. 1 with *What Do You Want?*), **Billy Fury** (*Maybe Tomorrow* and *Margot*), **Tony Newley** (*I've Waited So Long*, *Idle On Parade* EP and *Personality*), the late **Johnny Kidd** (*Please Don't Touch*), **Craig Douglas** (*A Teenager In Love* and a No. 1 with *Only 16*), **Dickie Pride** (*Primrose Lane*), **Clinton Ford** (*Old Shep*) and **Al Saxon** (*You're The Top Cha*, *Only 16*).

Elvis Presley (never a year without him) continued his military service for Uncle Sam but managed to keep up his million-sellers with *One Night*, *A Fool Such As I* and *A Big Hunk Of Love*. **Frankie Avalon** had *Venus* and *Just Ask Your Heart*, and **The Coasters** added humour with *Charlie Brown* and *Poison Ivy*.

Bobby Darin had big hits with *Dream Lover* and *Mack The Knife*, and **Paul Anka** with *Lonely Boy* and *Put Your Head On My Shoulder*. Newcomers **Lloyd Price** had *Stagger Lee* and *Personality*, **Neil Sedaka** *I Go Ape* and *Oh Carol* (back in the charts in 1972 and about Carol King), and film star **Fabian** with *Tiger*. **Guy Mitchell's** *Heartaches By The Number*, and **Fats Domino's** *Be My Guest* added to the beat.

The **Everly Brothers** 1959 hits were *Problems*, *Poor Jenny*, *Take A Message To Mary* and *(Til) I Kissed You*. **Ricky Nelson** had *Never Be Anyone Else But You* and *A Little Too Much*, and **Bobby Rydell** debuted with *We Got Love* and *Wild One*, while **Eddie Cochran** invited you to *C'Mon Everybody*.

Among the more tuneful world hits were **Brook Benton's** *Just A Matter Of Time*, **Johnny Mathis'** *Misty*, **Andy Williams'** *Hawaiian Wedding*, **Phil Phillips'** *Sea Of Love*, **Wilbert Harrison's** *Kansas City*, **Paul Evans'** *Seven Little Girls* (a hit for the **Avons** in Britain), **Jerry Keller's** *Here Comes Summer*, and **Jackie Wilson's** *Lonely Teardrop*.

In more boisterous vein were *What'd I Say* by **Ray Charles**;

The Everly Brothers had many hits in 1959

39

1
Cliff Richard

2
Adam Faith

3
Emile Ford

4
Tony Newley

Tallahassie Lassie and *Way Down Yonder In New Orleans* by **Freddie Cannon**; *Ships On A Stormy Sea* by **Jimmy Clanton** and **Henry Mancini's** jazz opus *Peter Gunn*.

Three novelty records were deejay **Wink Martindale's** recitation of *Deck Of Cards*; **Edd Byrnes** and **Connie Stevens** duet of *Kookie Lend Me Your Comb* (from the "77 Sunset Strip" TV show) and more **David Seville** Chipmunk songs — *Alvin's Harmonica* and *Ragtime Cowboy Joe*.

Marvin Rainwater continued to add Golds with *My Love Is Real, My Brand of Blue*, and *Half Breed*, and other country-and-western top hits were **Stonewall Jackson's** *Waterloo*, **Marty Robbins'** *El Paso*, the British team **Mike and Griff's** *Hold Back Tomorrow*, and **Johnny Horton's** *Battle of New Orleans*.

Lonnie Donegan won the *New Orleans* chart-battle from **Horton** in Britain and had a good year with further hits — *Does Your Chewing Gum Lose Its Flavour* (On The Bedpost Overnight?) was a million-seller by 1961, *Forth Worth Jail, Sal's Got A Sugar Lip* and *San Miguel*.

The girl vocalists were led by **Connie Francis** with *Who's Sorry Now, You Always Hurt The One You Love, My Happiness, Among My Souvenirs* and *Lipstick On Your Collar*, **Della Reece** with *Don't You Know*, **Nina Simone** with *I Love You Porgy* (from "Porgy And Bess"), **LaVerne Baker** with *I Cried A Tear*, **Sarah Vaughan** with *Broken Hearted Melody*, **Shirley Bassey** with *As I Love You, Kiss Me Honey Honey Kiss Me* and *If You Love Me*, and **Ruby Murray** with *Goodbye Jimmy Goodbye*.

Frank Sinatra made the Top Ten with *High Hopes* and **Tommy Steele** had a children's ditty called *Little White Bull*. And to add to the quieter era in pop, we had the **Harry Simeone Chorale** in the charts for several weeks with *Little Drummer Boy*.

A sad loss during the year was the death in a plane crash of **Buddy Holly, Ritchie Valens** and **Big Bopper** in North Dakota during a snow storm in February, when they were on tour.

2

1

1
Bobby Rydell

2
Julie Rogers and Billy Fury

3
The Chris Barber Band

4
Craig Douglas

5
Russ Conway

3

4

5

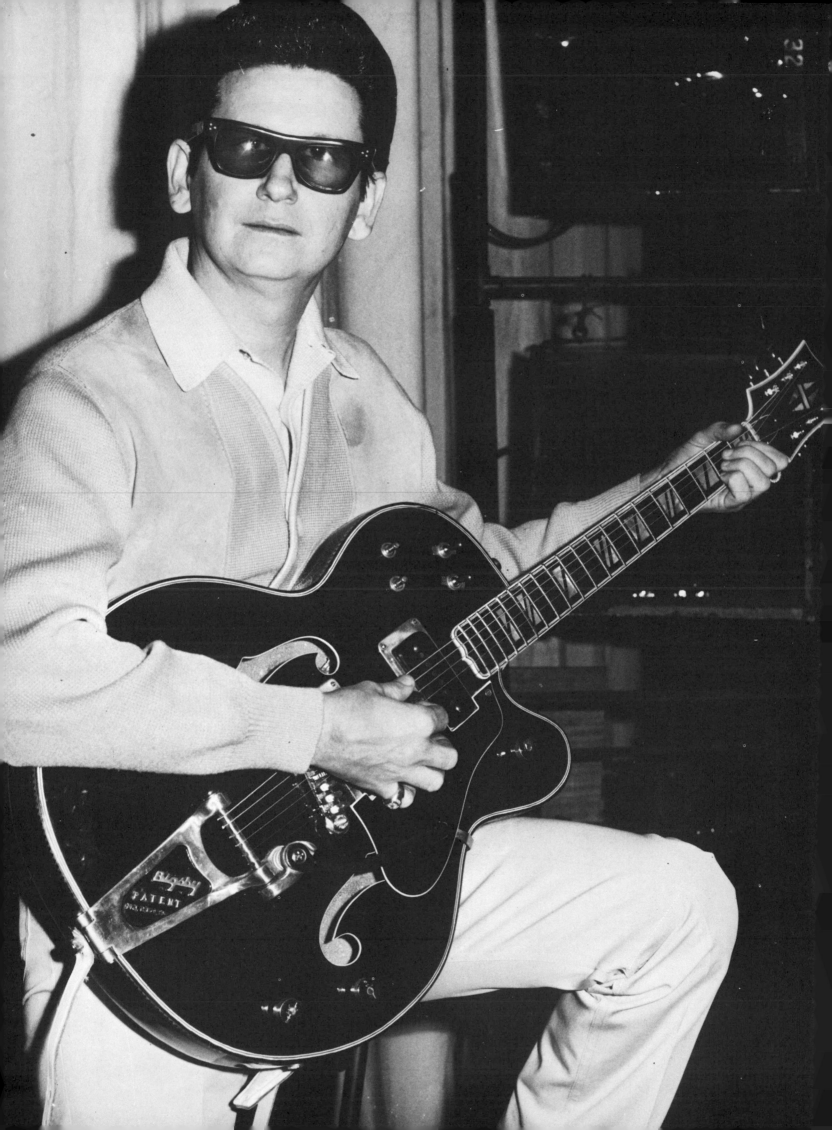

1960

The new decade opened quietly with wilder rock'n'roll on the decline. **Bill Haley**, **Little Richard** (retired to do evangelistic work) and others had disappeared from the charts. Songs still had an accented beat but more melody was infused into them and were known as beat-ballads.

Elvis Presley was still the leader, but even he resorted to a romantic Neopolitan classic composed in 1901, *O Sole Mio*, which was dressed up with a new English lyric and renamed *It's Now Or Never*, which is said to be his biggest ever seller, backed with a raver, *Stuck On You*. Two other strong ballads were *Wooden Heart* and *Are You Lonesome Tonight?* Elvis also had his third million-selling LP, from the film track of "GI Blues".

The most important newcomer of the year was **Roy Orbison**, a successful Nashville composer who sprang to fame singing his own *Only The Lonely*, in a sorrowful, wailing, intense voice. The **Everly Brothers**, who had a hit with Roy's *Claudette*, gave us a new big one in *Cathy's Clown* and other beat ballads which earned Gold Records in 1960 were **Johnny Tillotson's** *Poetry In Motion*, **Johnny Preston's** *Running Bear*, **Jack Scott's** *What In The World's Come Over You*, **Marv Johnson's** (You've Got To) *Move Two Mountains*, **Johnny Horton's** *North To Alaska*, **Perry Como's** *Delaware*, **Mark Dinning's** *Teen Angel*, **Conway Twitty's** *Lonely Blue Boy*, and the **Drifters'** *True Love/Dance With Me*, and *Save The Last Dance For Me*.

Duane Eddy's guitar won him more fame with *Because They're Young* and another top million-selling instrumental was *Apache*, from **The Shadows**, the British group which had started as **The Drifters** but changed its name because of the American group called that. Ironically, **The Shadows'** *Apache* toppled 'boss' **Cliff Richard**, for whom they started as a backing group, from the British No. 1 spot. Cliff's hit was *Please Don't Tease*, and others during the year that made him top of the popularity polls were *Travellin' Light*, *Voice In The Wilderness*, *Fall In Love With You*, *Nine Times Out Of Ten* and *I Love You*.

The Shadows got a shock when they discovered American star **Bobby Vee**, another important Gold newcomer of 1960, had a group called **The Shadows**, but they never gained the fame of the British group. However, **Bobby** had million-sellers with *Devil Or Angel* and *Rubber Ball* (and it's interesting to know he is still recording under his full name — **Robert Thomas Velline**).

Another instrumental group to make a 'million' debut was **The Ventures**, of California, with *Walk Don't Run*, the start of a non-stop career which still goes on. **Bill Black's Combo** continued with *White Silver Sands* and *Josephine*, while on the musical side, Themes were very popular — **Mantovani** with his "Exodus And Other Themes" LP (65 consecutive weeks in the U.S. LP charts), piano duettists **Ferrante and Teicher** with Theme from "The Apartment" (first of 14 million-sellers from F & T), and **Percy Faith** with Theme from "Summer Place". **Don Costa** had plenty of mandolins in his band for *Never On Sunday*.

The girls did well, newcomer **Brenda Lee**, aged 16, of Nashville, bowing in with *Sweet Nothin's*, a massive hit, and following with *I'm Sorry/That's All You Gotta Do*; **The Shirelles**, three New Jersey schoolgirls, debuting with a trio of Gold Records — *Dedicated To The One I Love*, *Tonight's The Night* and *Will You Love Me Tomorrow*; **Connie Stevens** with *Something Special*; **Anita Bryant** with *Paper Roses*; and **Connie Francis** having no fewer than four Golds in a year for *Mama/Teddy*, *Everybody's Somebody's Fool*, *Many Tears Ago*, and *My Heart Has A Mind Of Its Own*.

The late **Dinah Washington**, a beautiful singer of blues, duetted *Baby* with **Brook Benton** for a Gold, **Maurice Williams and the Zodiacs** had *Stay*, and **Jackie Wilson** continued with *Night/Doggin' Around*.

Lonnie Donegan became the first British artist to have three million-sellers when his *My Old Man's A Dustman* won him a Gold Record. **Ray Charles** added *Georgia On My Mind*, and **Paul Anka** had *Puppy Love* and *My Home Town*. Newcomer **Johnny Burnette** gave us *You're 16*, **Sam Cooke** added *Wonderful World* and *Chain Gang*, and **Bobby Darin's** latest Gold was *Beyond The Sea* (La Mer). That amazing piano-vocal man **Fats Domino** got his 22nd million-seller with *Walkin' To New Orleans/Don't Keep Knockin'*. A Nashville pianist, **Floyd Cramer**, scored with *Last Date*, and the harmonising **Brothers Four** with *Green Fields*.

A new dance craze was starting, *The Twist*, which was the title of the record to bring the chief twister, **Chubby Checker**, his first Gold Record. The **Hollywood Argyles** gave us the novel *Alley Oop*, and

Roy Orbison made his mark in 1960 with *Only The Lonely*

1
The Shadows

2
Jimmy Jones

3
Chubby Checker

a young New Yorker, **Brian Hyland**, had a big one with *Itsy Bitsy Teenie Weenie Yellow Polka Dot Bikini!* Another newcomer, **Jimmy Jones**, had two tuneful hits – *Handy Man* and *Good Timin'*, while **Bobby Rydell** gave us the first *Ding-A-Ling* hit.

In Britain, **Adam Faith** had a very good year with five hits – *Poor Baby* (No. 1), *Someone Else's Baby*, *Made You*, *When Johnny Comes Marching Home* and *How About That*, while his co-star at Blackpool in the summer, **Emile Ford**, had *Slow Boat To China*, *Lucky Old Sun*, *You'll Never Know What You're Missing* and *Them There Eyes*. Few of the established girl singers had hits, but **Shirley Bassey** won fame with *As Long As He Needs Me* and newcomer **Maureen Evans** did well with *The Big Hurt*.

Acker Bilk's haunting clarinet made *Summer Set* a major favourite and the instrumental **John Barry Seven** put *Hit And Miss* in the charts. **Joe Brown** *(Darktown Strutters Ball)*, **Ricky Valence** *(Tell Laura I Love Her)* and **Frank Ifield** *(Lucky Devil)* had first hits.

Comedian **Ken Dodd** started his run of record successes with *Love Is Like A Violin*, and Australian all-rounder **Rolf Harris** made the charts with *Tie Me Kangaroo Down Sport*. **Donald Peers**, a major star ten years before, came back with *Papa Love Mama*, and French star **Edith Piaf** got in with *Milord*, which **Frankie Vaughan** shared.

No. 1 hits came from **Michael Holliday's** *Starry Eyed*, and **Tony Newley's** *Why* and *Do You Mind*. Other big ones were **Elvis Presley's** *Mess Of Blues*, **Duane Eddy's** *Shazam*, **Johnny Preston's** *Cradle Of Love*, **Michael Cox's** *Angela Jones*, **Garry Mills'** *Look For A Star*, and a novelty by **Peter Sellers** and **Sophia Loren** called *Goodness Gracious Me*.

The tragedy of the year was the death of **Eddie Cochran** in a car crash near Bath in April. **Gene Vincent** was injured with him. Eddie had *C'Mon Everybody*, *Something Else*, *Hallelujah I Love Her So* and, ironically, *Three Steps To Heaven* as his big hits.

2

1

1
Connie Stevens

2
Johnny Tillotson

3
Richie Valence

4
Frank Ifield

5
Acker Bilk

6
Dinah Washington

7
Brenda Lee

8
Bobby Vee

7

8

5

6

1961

Trad jazz, **Helen Shapiro**, the Twist, the beginning of Tamla Motown, more million-selling LPs — these were the outstanding features of 1961.

Trad and **Helen Shapiro** weren't purely British happenings, either. They were international. The big three of the Trad revival, which came from the Mississippi delta and New Orleans, were London-based **Acker Bilk**, **Kenny Ball** and **Chris** (Petite Fleur) **Barber**. **Acker's** million-seller, admittedly, was a softy called Stranger On The Shore, of which his clarinet solo was backed by the **Leon Young String Chorale**, but it was the exception, because other hits the Somerset wildcat had were Buona Sera, That's My Home and Creole Jazz, all fast, jerky, happy numbers.

Kenny Ball's Gold Disc was a trad arrangement of a Russian melody, Midnight In Moscow, and other 1961 hits were Samantha, I Still Love You All and Someday. Other trad bands in great demand were those of **Terry Lightfoot** (True Love, King Kong), **Bob Wallis**, **Alex Welsh**, **Dick Charlesworth**, **Mike Cotton**, **Alan Elsdon**, **Monty Sunshine** (who left **Chris Barber**), **Charlie Galbraith** and **The Temperance Seven**, which really was a burlesque-of-the-1930s band, winning fans with You're Driving Me Crazy.

Helen Shapiro, aged 14 and still a North London schoolgirl with a rather deep, attractive voice and a great sense of rhythm, was the answer to record producer Norrie Paramor's prayer. He wanted a girl singer who could sing beat numbers. Helen was a pupil of the Maurice Burman singing school, Maurice being a popular vocalist of the '30s but who died suddenly before Helen's success. She had world hits with You Don't Know and Walking Back To Happiness during the year.

Another British act won world acclaim with a self-written song, Are You Sure? They were **The Allisons**, of London — John and Bob, not brothers, just friends, and they had the one major hit. To add to Britain's flock of Golds, **Petula Clark** got one for Romeo, and she also had a hit with Ya Ya, a million-seller for **Lee Dorsey**.

Chubby Checker continued to get everyone twisting with Pony Time, Let's Twist Again and The Fly, while **Joey Dee and The Starliters** did the same with Peppermint Twist. Films featuring twist and trad were popular.

More newcomers to gain Golds were **Gary U.S. Bonds**, a rock singer from Florida, with Quarter To Three, **Dee Clark** with Raindrops, film actor **James Darren** with Goodbye Cruel World, country-and-western singer **Jimmy Dean** with Big Bad John, a duet-team, **Dick and Deedee**, with The Mountain's High, and **The Highwaymen** with Michael Row The Boat Ashore, which several artists covered.

No. 1s in both America and Britain were **Bobby Lewis**, from an Indiannapolis orphanage, with Tossin' And Turnin', four Pittsburg youngsters called **The Marcels** with Blue Moon, and **Del Shannon**, from Grand Rapids, Michigan, with Runaway, followed by Hats Off To Larry.

Tamla Motown was just starting out in Detroit in 1961 and founder **Berry Gordy Jr.** was behind their first two million-sellers — **The Marvelettes**, five girls, with Please Mister Postman, and **The Miracles**, four men and a girl, led by **Smokey Robinson**, who wrote Shop Around, with Gordy. The label became one of the most successful ever in pop history.

More new acts to gain first Gold Records were **The Dovells**, from Philadelphia, with Bristol Stomp; **Gene McDaniel** with One Hundred Pounds Of Clay; the **Mar-Keys**, of Memphis, with Last Night, and bass-player **Bob Moore and his Orchestra** with a novelty called Mexico. **Gene Pitney** made his bow with Town Without Pity, and **Linda Scott** had I've Told Every Little Star. The instrumental number Wheels gave the **String-a-Longs** and **Billy Vaughn** Gold Discs (and **Joe Loss** a hit as Wheels Cha Cha), and **Sue Thompson** had two from Sad Movies and Norman. **The Tokens**, five Brooklyn boys, made a Zulu song called Wimoweh into a Gold Record, re-titled The Lion Sleeps Tonight.

Those who added more Gold Records to their collection in 1961 were **Pat Boone** (Moody River), **Ray Charles** (Hit The Road Jack), **Floyd Cramer** (On The Rebound), **Brook Benton** (Boll Weevil Song), **Dion** (Runaround Sue — without The Belmonts), **The Everly Brothers** (Walk Right Back), **Ferrante and Teicher** (Tonight), **Connie Francis** (Where The Boys Are and Together), **Ricky Nelson** (Hello Mary Lou/Travellin' Man), **Sandy Nelson** (Let There Be Drums), **Roy Orbison** (Runnin' Scared and Cryin'), **Bobby Vee** (Take Good Care Of My Baby) and **The Ventures** (Perfidia).

Elvis Presley, naturally, continued to dominate the hit parades with Surrender, I Feel So Bad, Little Sister/His Latest Flame, and Can't Help

Helen Shapiro was a 14-year-old wonder of 1961

Falling In Love With You/ Rock-a-Hula Baby. He also had an LP million-seller of the "Blue Hawaii" film soundtrack.

Three other top-selling albums of 1961 were the "West Side Story" film LP, which stayed in world LP charts for nearly four years; "**Judy Garland** At The Carnegie Hall", a double-album, in-performance set which sold a million copies in four years, and **Mantovani's** *Italia Mio.*

An interesting, German-made record which became a million-seller by 1964 was *My Bonnie/When The Saints Go Marching In,* sung by a Norwich-born rocker called **Tony Sheridan** and backed by a group called **The Beatles**! But in 1961 they were almost unknown outside their native Liverpool and their adopted Hamburg.

Well-known in Britain, however, were **Eden Kane's** *Well I Ask You,* **John Leyton's** *Johnny Remember Me* and *Wild Wind,* **Matt Monro's** *Portrait Of My Love* and *My Kind Of Girl,* **Cliff Richard's** *Girl In My Arms, Gee Whiz It's You* and *Theme For A Dream,* **The Shadows'** *Kon Tiki* and *FBI,* **Danny Williams'** *Moon River,* **Billy Fury's** *Halfway To Paradise,* **Adam Faith's** *Who Am I?,* and **Shirley Bassey's** *Reach For The Stars* and *Climb Every Mountain.* A new act called **The Springfields** had a first with *Breakaway,* and interesting chart races were between **Bobby Vee** and **Marty Wilde** for *Rubber Ball* honours, and **Petula Clark** and **Anne Shelton** for *Sailor.* Finally, "The Young Ones", starring **Cliff Richard**, was hailed as the best British musical for years.

Gene Pitney

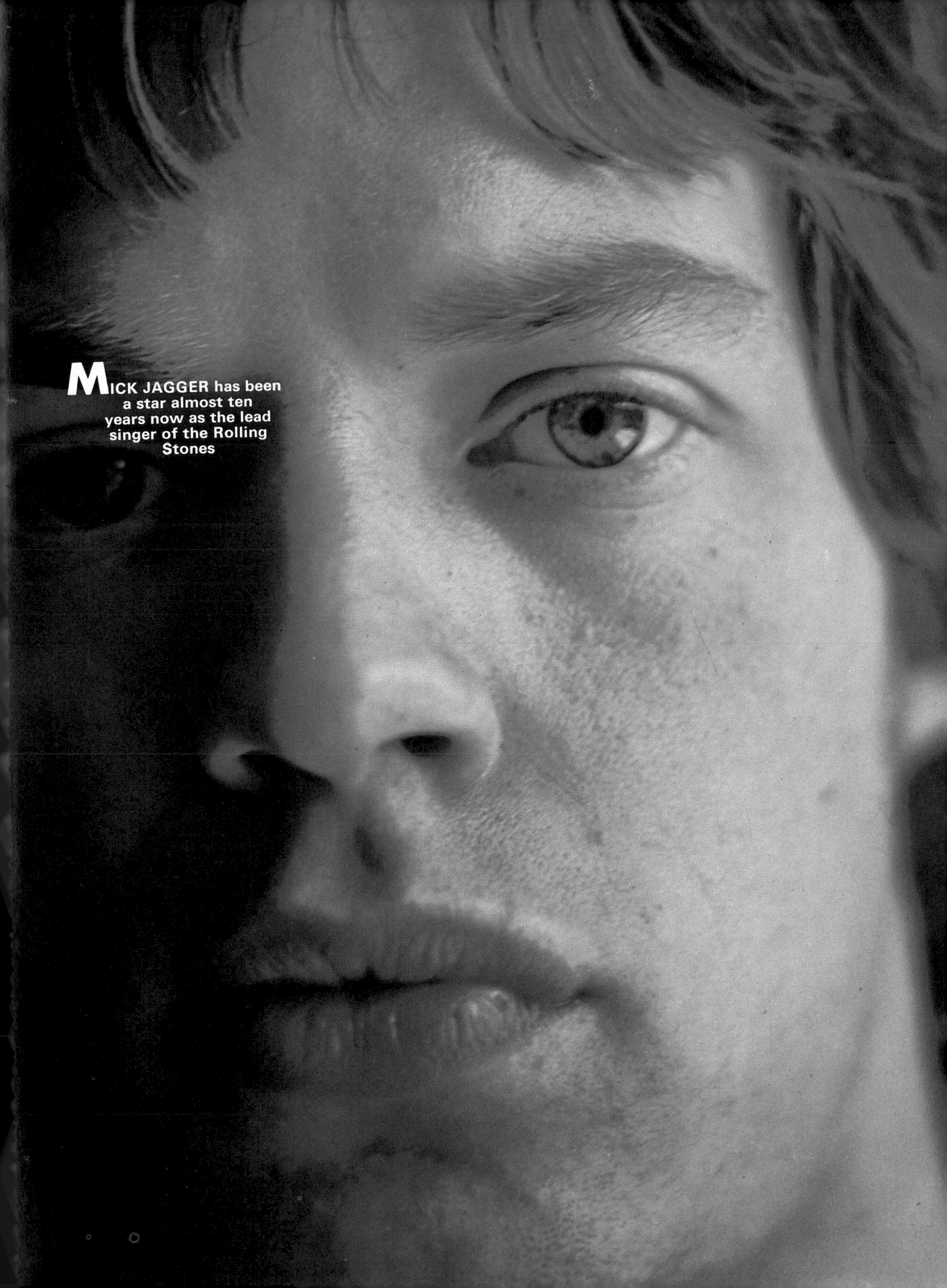

MICK JAGGER has been a star almost ten years now as the lead singer of the Rolling Stones

DONOVAN was Britain's reply to Bob Dylan when he got a hit with his song *Sunshine Superman*

Elvis Presley in Germany in
1960

1
Del Shannon

2
Kenny Ball

3
Judy Garland

4
John Leyton, with Jennifer
Jones in "The Idol"

5
Matt Monro and Dusty
Springfield

6
Eden Kane

7
The Miracles

5

6

7

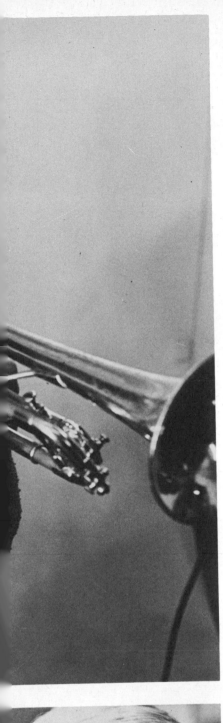

1962

This was a year in which all sorts of records won Gold Discs for million sales, the lull before the great breakout of **The Beatles**, who had their first solo chart entry in 1962 with *Love Me Do* – at No. 27 for one week only. It disappeared the next week and never made a re-appearance in the British single charts, though it became a million-seller in America in 1964.

The only British artists to make million-sellers during the year were **Frank Ifield**, born in England and from Australia, with *I Remember You* and *Lovesick Blues*, **Petula Clark** with *Monsieur* (sales mostly in Germany) and *Chariot* (big sales in France), **Cliff Richard** with *The Young Ones* and *Bachelor Boy/The Next Time*, **The Shadows** with *Wonderful Land*, and a new group of five session musicians, **The Tornados**, with *Telstar*, which was No. 1 in Britain for five weeks and in America for three.

In America there were plenty of new million-sellers produced – **Elvis Presley** leading with *Good Luck Charm/Anything That's Part Of You*, *She's Not You*, and *Return To Sender* – all chart-toppers in both America and Britain.

A Californian trumpet player, **Herb Alpert**, 25, made an instrumental record called *Lonely Bull*, with a Tijuana (Mexico) sound, for 200 dollars and sold a million copies, starting a major recording company called A & M. Other mainly instrumental Golds were **Booker T and The MGs** (for Memphis Group) with *Green Onions*; **Joey Dee and The Starliters** with *Shout*; **Duane Eddy's** (Dance With) *The Guitar Man*; **David Rose's** *The Stripper*; and tenor sax **Stan Getz** and jazz guitarist **Charlie Byrd** with bossa-novas *Desafinado* and *Jazz Samba*.

Vocal group successes became more numerous with **The Four Seasons'** *Sherry* and *Big Girls Don't Cry*; **The Orlons'** *Wah-Watusi* and *Don't Hang Up*; folk singing **Peter, Paul and Mary** with an LP named after them, Texans **Paul and Paula** with *Hey Paula*; **The Shirelles** with *Soldier Boy*; **The Contours** with *Do You Love Me*; and **Bobby (Boris) Pickett** and **The Crypt Kickers** with *Monster Mash!*

Country songs gave rhythm-and-blues singer **Ray Charles** his most successful album, *Modern Sounds Of Country-And-Western Music*, which was No. 1 in America for 18 weeks and in the American LP chart for two years. Ray had a monster single from it, *I Can't Stop Loving You*, and later *You Don't Know Me*, while another coloured singer, **Nat King Cole** had another c & w orientated Gold LP with *Rambling Rose*, which also was a very big hit single. Country singers with million-sellers were **Ned Miller** (*From A Jack To A King*), **Skeeter Davis** (*The End Of The World*) and **Claude King** (*Wolverton Mountain*).

Popular vocalists continued to meet the challenge of groups. **Tony Bennett** gave us his greatest hit, *I Left My Heart In San Francisco*, **Sammy Davis Jr.** sang Anthony Newley's *What Kind Of Fool Am I?*, **Bobby Darin** had *Things*, **Shelley Fabares** (*Johnny Angel*), **Steve Lawrence** (*Go Away Little Girl*), **Brenda Lee** (*All Alone Am I*), **Ketty Lester** (*Love Letters*), **Gene Pitney** (*Man Who Shot Liberty Valance, If I Didn't Have A Dime/One Love Can't Break A Heart*), **Roy Orbison** (*Dream Baby*), **Bobby Vee** (*Night Had A Thousand Eyes*), **Neil Sedaka** (*Breaking Up Is Hard To Do*) and **Andy Williams** (*Moon River And Other Themes* LP, four years in US LP charts).

New young rockers on the scene were **Chris Montez** with *Let's Dance* and *Some Kinda Fun*, **Little Eva** with *Loco-Motion*, **Gene Chandler** with *Hey Baby*, **Tommy Roe** with *Sheila*, **Dee Dee Sharp** with *Mashed Potato Time* and *Ride*, and **Bobby Vinton** with *Roses Are Red*. More established rockers added Golds – **Isley Brothers** (*Twist And Shout*), **Freddy Cannon** (*Palisades Park*) and **Brian Hyland** with *Sealed With A Kiss*.

Twist interest waned towards the end of the year, but not before **Chubby Checker** had two more Golds from *Slow Twist* and *Limbo Rock/Popeye*, **Sam Cooke** had *Twisting The Night Away* and **Frank Sinatra** changed *Everybody's Truckin'* into *Everybody's Twistin'*. Comedy came from **Pat Boone's** *Speedy Gonzales*, **Ray Stevens'** *Ahab The Arab*, **Lou Monte's** *Pepino The Italian Mouse*, and **Vaughn Meader's** take-off of "The First Family" (President John Kennedy). Clever parodies made **Allan Sherman** famous, the first being *My Son The Folk Singer*.

A novelty of the year was the first Japanese artist to break through world-wide, **Kyu Sakamoto**, with the plaintive *Sukiyaki*, which got to No. 1 in America in 1963 and was a hit on Britain, too, where **Helen Shapiro** was the young Queen, topping the bill at the London Palladium, starring on Ed Sullivan's nationwide American TV show, which gave wide fame to **Elvis Presley** and **The Beatles** first in

Herb Alpert made the Tijuana sound a best-seller in 1962

1
Craig Douglas

2
Frank Ifield

America, and making a world tour — all at the age of 15! Her big record was *Tell Me What He Said*.

British No. 1 records were **Elvis'** million-sellers already mentioned, **The Shadows'** *Wonderful Land*, **Cliff Richard's** *The Young Ones*, **B. Bumble And The Stingers'** *Nut Rocker*, **Mike Sarne's** *Come Outside*, **Chubby Checker's** *Let's Twist Again*, **Frank Ifield's** *Lovesick Blues* and *I Remember You*, **Joe Brown's** *Picture Of You*, and **Carole King's** *Rain Until September*.

Other big favourites were **The Springfields'** *Silver Threads And Golden Needles*, **Del Shannon's** *Swiss Maid*, **Craig Douglas'** *Oh Lonesome Me*, **Duane Eddy's** *Deep In The Heart Of Texas*, **Tommy Steele's** *Put A Ring On Her Finger* and **Jimmy Justice's** *Spanish Harlem*.

LP sales increased so much in Britain that album charts were published alongside single charts. In the first "New Musical Express" LP chart on June 8, 1962, were four film soundtrack albums — 1. Blue Hawaii (**Presley** film), 2. West Side Story, 3. It's Trad Dad, 4. South Pacific, 5. The Young Ones — **Cliff Richard and The Shadows**, 6. I Remember Tommy (Dorsey) — **Frank Sinatra**, 7. Sinatra And Strings — **Frank Sinatra**, 8. Black And White Minstrel Show, 9. Sound Of Music — London Cast, and 10. Honey Hit Parade — Various Artists.

This chart proves how popular **Frank Sinatra** was (and still is) on albums. The two mentioned above were on his own Reprise label, but he was at one time issued on seven different labels and selling well on all of them. Another LP feat was the issue of a 15-album set called **Bing Crosby's** Hollywood, featuring 186 film tunes from 44 pictures from 1934—56, eleven hours of playing time!

1

1
Kyu Sakamoto

2
Peter, Paul and Mary

3
Carole King

4
Chris Montez

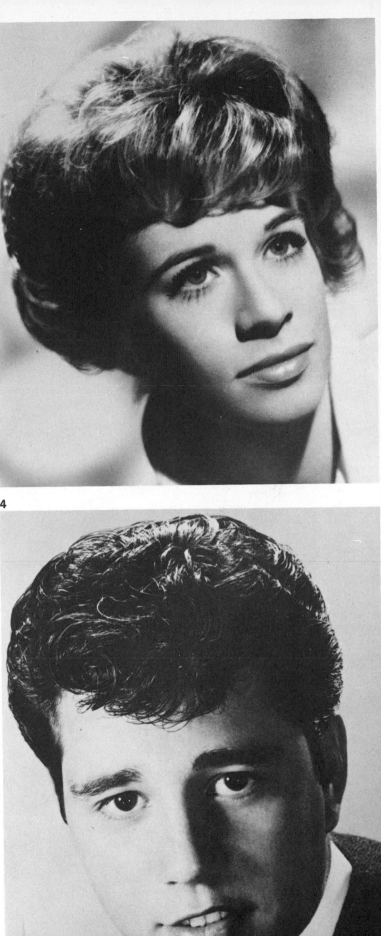

1
Tommy Roe

2
Nat King Cole

3
Booker T and The MGs

4
The Tornados

5
Little Eva

6
Cliff Richard and The Shadows

1963

What a great year for British pop music! **The Beatles** carried all before them — selling an estimated seven million records in the United Kingdom alone. They also sold all over Europe, America and the rest of the world, but didn't go to, and conquer, America until the following year.

They had colossal single hits with *She Loves You, From Me To You* and *I Want To Hold Your Hand* (these songs occupied the top of the the British charts for 18 weeks during the year), they had extended-play (four tunes) record hits, and two No. 1 LPs. Everything became million-sellers and more for them. They appeared in the Royal Variety Show, and after supporting **Helen Shapiro**, then **Tommy Roe-Chris Montez** and later **Roy Orbison**, became stars of their own shows from July.

Liverpudlians **John Lennon**, rhythm guitar, 22, and **Paul McCartney**, bass guitar, 20, were the songwriters of the group and **George Harrison**, lead guitar, 19, was the musician, while **Ringo Starr**, 22, was the happy drummer, replacing **Pete Best** in 1962. Paul, John and George became **The Quarrymen** skiffle group in 1956 when still at school, then the **Silver Beatles** at the Star Club, Hamburg, and Cavern Club, Liverpool, where they appeared nearly 300 times. They backed **Johnny Gentle** in Scotland in 1960 and made a record in Germany with **Tony Sheridan** (see 1961).

Brian Epstein, a young Liverpool businessman with a record shop, became **The Beatles'** manager in 1962 and started to organise their haphazard career. George Martin, of EMI, became their record producer, and Dick James, a former singer, their music publisher. Their music was called Merseybeat, happy, simple, tuneful, singable stuff.

By the end of 1963, they had at No. 1 *I Want To Hold Your Hand* and 2. *Please Please Me*, and No. 1 *With The Beatles* and 2. *Please Please Me* LP in the singles and album charts respectively of the "New Musical Express".

Their success started a welter of Merseybeat vocal-instrumental groups. From Liverpool — **Billy J. Kramer and The Dakotas** (they made *Do You Want To Know A Secret* a hit before **The Beatles** had it, and *Bad To Me*, written by John and Paul), **Gerry and The Pacemakers** (*How Do You Do It?, I Like It* and *You'll Never Walk Alone* — all No. 1s), **The Big Three** (*By The Way*), **The Searchers** (*Sweets For My Sweet*), **The Foremost** (*Hello Little Girl*), **The Swinging Blue Jeans** (*It's Too Late Now*); from Manchester — the comic **Freddie and The Dreamers** (*If You Gotta Make A Fool Of Somebody, I'm Telling You Now, You Were Made For Me*) and **Hollies** (*Searchin'*); from London — **Dave Clark Five** (*Glad All Over, Do You Love Me*) and **Brian Poole and The Tremeloes** (*Twist And Shout* — in competition with **Beatles** and **Isley Brothers**; and *Do You Love Me* — Trems had the hit in Britain, **Dave Clark Five** in America); from East Anglia — **Bern Elliott and The Fenman** (*Money* — Bern is now in **Hollies**). Groups occupied No. 1 positions in the British charts for 39 weeks of the year.

Yet another British group, nothing to do with Merseybeat, but with a rhythm-and-blues basis, made its first chart entry — **The Rolling Stones** with *Come On*. And **Dusty Springfield** made a solo hit with *I Only Want To Be With You* after The Springfields broke up. **Cilla Black**, friend of the **Beatles** and a Liverpool singer, made it with *Love Of The World* and **Kathy Kirby** broke in with *Dance On* and *Secret Love*. **Heinz** also made a chart debut with *Dreams Do Come True*, after leaving the Tornados. **Mickie Most**, now a top producer and record company owner (Rak), had a hit with *Mr. Porter* and **Dave Berry** with *Memphis Tennessee*. **Jet Harris** and **Tony Meehan**, ex-Shadows, had a big hit with *Scarlett O'Hara*.

Cliff Richard and The Shadows had a good year with *Lucky Lips* and *Don't Talk To Him*, as well as several top LPs. Cliff was voted Top World Singer in the "New Musical Express" popularity poll, toppling **Elvis Presley**, who nonetheless had three more million-sellers in 1963 — *Devil In Disguise, Bossa Nova Baby* and *One Broken Heart For Sale*, but the rather poor films he kept making quickly in Hollywood weren't helping his popularity (though he topped the poll from 1957 to 1973 except for 1963!).

Other big British hits were **Frank Ifield's** *I'm Confessin'* and **Shirley Bassey's** *I Who Have Nothing* — both No. 1 hits, and **Kenny Lynch's** *You Can Never Stop Me Loving You*. **Jim Reeves** stayed nine weeks in the chart with *Welcome To My World*.

A novelty was a pretty little ditty, *Dominique*, sung by Sister Sourire, who became known to the world as **The Singing Nun**. A Belgian singing in French, she added a million-selling LP to it. Surfing was the subject of four Gold Discs by **The Beach Boys** (*Surfin' USA* and *Surfer Girl*), **Jan and Dean** (*Surf City*) and **The Surfaris** (*Wipe Out*)

The Beatles led the great British pop revival in 1963

1
Trini Lopez

2
Cilla Black

3
The Rolling Stones

4
Dionne Warwicke

5
**Billy J. Kramer (centre)
and The Dakotas**

— all of California.

Vocal groups continued to multiply in America. Girl groups with million-sales were three from New York — **The Angels** *(My Boyfriend's Back)*, **The Chiffons** *(He's So Fine)*, **The Crystals** *(Da Doo Ron Ron)*, **Martha and The Vandellas** *(Heatwave)*, **The Ronettes** *(Be My Baby)*, and male or mixed groups were **The Essex** *(Easier Said Than Done)*, **The Cascades** *(Rhythm Of The Rain)*, Texan **Jimmy Gilmore and The Fireballs** *(Sugar Shack)*, **The Kingsmen**, of Portland, Oregon *(Louie Louie)*, **Garrett Minns and The Enchanters** *(Cry Baby)*, **The New Christie Minstrels** *(Green Green)*, **The Rooftop Singers** *(Walk Right In)* and **The Tymes** *(So Much In Love)*.

New American singers emerged to win Gold Discs, too — **Little Stevie Wonder**, a 12-year-old blind coloured vocalist-harmonica player signed to Tamla, with *Fingertips*; country-and-western singer **Bobby Bare** with *Detroit City*, **Inez Foxx** with *Mocking Bird*, **Lesley Gore** with *It's My Party*, **Dionne Warwick** with *Anyone Who Had A Heart*, the first of several Bacharach and David compositions she made famous; **Eydie Gorme** with *Blame It On The Bossa Nova*, **Mary Wells** with *Two Lovers*, **Little Peggy March** with *I Will Follow You*, **Trini Lopez** with a Latin-American version of *If I Had A Hammer*, **Bobby Bland** with *Call On Me*, and **Jimmy Soul** with *If You Wanna Be Happy*.

Established artists added more Gold Records to their collection — **The Drifters** *(Up On The Roof)*, **Ray Charles** *(Take These Chains From My Heart)*, **The Four Seasons** *(Walk Like A Man)*, **Andy Williams** *(Can't Get Used To Losing You)*, **Brenda Lee** *(Losing You)*, **Bobby Vinton** *(Blue Velvet* and *There I've Said It Again)*, **Roy Orbison** *(In Dreams* and *Mean Woman Blues)*, **The Orlons** *(South Street)* and **Gene Pitney** *(24 Hours To Tulsa)*.

But it was Britain in the ascendancy in 1963 and even more so in 1964.

1
The Beach Boys

2
Gerry and the Pacemakers
(Gerry Marsden in the
foreground)

1

2

BOBBIE GENTRY sprang to fame in 1967 with her own composition *Ode To Billie Joe*

JIMI HENDRIX, the American guitar genius who found fame in Britain, where he died in 1970

1

2

1
The Hollies

2
The Dave Clark Five (Dave Clark on the left)

1
Joe Brown

2
Freddie (Garrity, centre)
and the Dreamers

3
The Searchers

4
Jim Reeves

Mick Jagger, singer of The Rolling Stones, who shot to the top in 1964

1964

This was Britain's year! The year that America paid more attention to British pop music than its own! And British charts were filled with British, not American, records. The entire young world looked at Britain as the leaders, and Swinging London became their capital of the globe.

After the **Beatles** went on American television — with Ed Sullivan, of course, the man who had launched **Elvis Presley** — and toured triumphantly through the States, other British acts followed and anything British in records, clothes and other teen fads were "in" and the hitherto American domination of such things was over.

This bolstered the British coffers with sorely needed dollars at a time when they were much required and Harold Wilson, then Prime Minister, awarded MBEs to all four **Beatles**. Pop was becoming posh! (But **John Lennon** later returned his MBE.) The Variety Club's Silver Hearts for the Personalities of the Year, the Carl-Alan Awards, five Ivor Novello Awards and every Pop Poll Award came their way. British group dominance still persists, with our top small bands playing to packed houses all across America.

The **Beatles** themselves were never over-confident of their appeal. I remember **Paul McCartney**, the **Beatles'** Press spokesman, saying: "I suppose America is our biggest challenge. It would knock us out to go over there and make good. And our first feature film is our second challenge in 1964." They went to America in February and were amazed at the welcome they got. Their New York hotel was besieged, their TV show in which they sang six numbers brought glowing reviews, their one and only concert in Washington was a riot and led to a return in July for a 24-city tour and lots more TV, keeping them in America until September.

The **Beatles** continued their Midas touch, everything they recorded turning to Gold. Their 1964 tally was *Can't Buy Me Love*, *Hard Day's Night*, *I Feel Fine/ She's A Woman*, and *Long Tall Sally* EP, plus seven LPs and one double-LP!

Another group which got the young girls going mad with excitement wherever they appeared was **The Rolling Stones**, with thick-lipped **Mick Jagger** doing jerky body movements as he sang and played harmonica all over the stage. The Stones were the first to wear what they liked on stage. They had uniforms but kept forgetting to take them to theatres. It was the start of the wear-what-you-like pop era. They entered the charts with *Not Fade Away* and later went straight into the charts at No. 1 with *Little Red Rooster*.

On March 24, 1964, for the first time ever the "New Musical Express" singles chart had an all-British Top Ten:

1. *Anyone Who Had A Heart* — **Cilla Black***
2. *Bits And Pieces* — **Dave Clark Five***
3. *Diane* — **The Bachelors***
4. *I Think Of You* — **The Merseybeats**
5. *Needles And Pins* — **The Searchers***
6. *Not Fade Away* — **The Rolling Stones***
7. *Little Children* — **Billy J. Kramer and The Dakotas***
8. *I'm The One* — **Gerry and The Pacemakers**
9. *Candy Man* — **Brian Poole and The Tremeloes**
10. *Boys Cry* — **Eden Kane**

(* became million-sellers)

Not a **Beatle** record! But they were soon back at No. 1 again, and at that time had 1 and 2 in the U.S. charts.

In 1964 the list of new Gold Discs contained more British than American records. New British groups to sell a million were **The Animals**, from Newcastle-on-Tyne, with *House Of The Rising Sun*; **Georgie Fame and The Blue Flames** with *Yeh Yeh*; **Herman's Hermits**, from Manchester, with young actor **Peter Noone** as lead singer Herman and a hit with *I'm Into Something Good*; **The Kinks**, from London, with *You Really Got Me* (**Ray Davies** is the leader and composer of their hits); more Londoners, **The Honeycombs**, with a girl drummer and *Have I The Right?* as their hit; **Manfred Mann**, a London quintet with organist Manfred himself from South Africa, two Golds with *Do Wah Diddy Diddy* and *Sha La La*; **The Moody Blues**, from Birmingham, with *Go Now*; **Sounds Orchestral**, featuring pianist **Johnny Pearson**, with *Cast Your Fate To The Wind*; and **The Zombies**, from Hertfordshire, with *She's Not There*.

Two singing groups to win Golds were **The Bachelors**, three Dublin boys, with *Diane* and *I Believe* (they made their first chart entry in 1963 with *Charmaine*), and **Peter** (Asher) **and Gordon** (Waller) with *World Without Love*, by **John Lennon** and **Paul McCartney**, and *Nobody I Know* — Peter and Gordon became very popular in America and today Peter is a major record producer in California.

1
Millie

2
Julie Rogers

3
The Beatles, with an M.B.E. each

4
Louis Armstrong

5
Lulu

6
The Nashville Teens

7
The Yardbirds

More established groups to add Golds were **Billy J. Kramer and The Dakotas** (*Little Children*), **The Searchers** (*Needles And Pins*), **Gerry and The Pacemakers** (*Don't Let The Sun Catch You Crying*), **Freddie and The Dreamers** (*I Understand*), and **The Dave Clark Five**, who became one of the biggest groups in America, along with Herman's Hermits, and had no less than four million-sellers — *Bits And Pieces, Can't You See That She Is Mine, Because*, and *Any Way You Want Me*.

Girl singers did very well in the million-selling stakes — **Mary Wells'** *My Guy*, **Dionne Warwick's** *Walk On By*, Britain's **Julie Rogers** with *The Wedding*, **Millie**, 16, from Jamaica, with *My Boy Lollipop*, **Petula Clark** with *Downtown*, **Shirley Bassey** with *Goldfinger*, **Cilla Black** with *Anyone Who Had A Heart* and *You're My World*, the American **Shangri-Las** (four girls) with *Remember* and *Leader Of The Pack*, **The Dixie Cups**, three New Orleans girls, with *Chapel Of Love*, and **The Supremes**, three Detroit girls led by **Diana Ross**, with three hits — *Where Did Our Love Go, Baby Love* and *Come See About Me*. **The Supremes** are still most popular today and **Diana Ross** is a major solo singer-film star.

New American male groups to win Gold Records were **Gary Lewis and The Playboys** (*This Diamond Ring*), **The Newbeats**, from Georgia (*Bread And Butter*), **The Righteous Brothers** (who were not brothers) with *You've Lost That Loving Feeling*; while established groups — **The Beach Boys** (*I Get Around* and *Fun Fun Fun*) and **The Four Seasons** (*Rag Doll*) also won Golds.

American solo singers gained fewer million-sellers, but **Lorne Green**, of "Bonanza" TV fame, had a hit called *Ringo*, as did **Dean Martin** (*Everybody Loves Somebody*), country-and-western singer **Roger Miller** (*Dang Me* and *Chug-a-Lug*), **Roy Orbison** (*Oh Pretty Woman* and *It's Over*), **Jim Reeves** (*I Love You Because* and *I Won't Forget You*), **Del Shannon** (*Keep Searchin'*), 64-year-old trumpeter-vocalist **Louis Armstrong** (*Hello Dolly*), and, of course, **Elvis Presley**, billed in film publicity as 'the original Beatle', had three more — *Viva Las Vegas, Kissin' Cousins*, and *Ain't That Lovin' You Baby*.

The two million-selling soundtrack albums both featured **Julie Andrews** — "Mary Poppins" and "My Fair Lady".

Not quite in the million-selling bracket, but doing very well in 1964 were these other chart-making British groups — **The Applejacks**, from Birmingham, with *Tell Me When*; the Salvation Army's **Joy Strings** group with *It's An Open Secret*, Liverpool's **Four Pennies** with *Juliet*, **The Mojos** with *Everything's All Right*, **The Downliner Sect** with *Baby What's Wrong*, **The Yardbirds** with *I Wish You Would*, **The Barron Knights** with a take-off of other groups in *Call Up The Groups* (to National Service), **The Nashville Teens'** *Tobacco Road*, **Wayne Fontana and The Mindbenders'** *Um Um Um*, **The Rockin' Berries'** *He's In Town*, **The Pretty Things'** *Don't Bring Me Down*, and **The Poets**, from Scotland, with *Now We're Through*.

Lulu made her chart debut with *Shout* and **P. J. Proby** made his with *Hold Me*. Other newcomers were **Marianne Faithfull** (*As Tears Go By*), **Sandie Shaw** (*Always Something There To Remind Me*) which was four weeks at No. 1, **Val Doonican** (*Walk Tall*), **Tommy Quickly** (*Wilde Side of Life*), and **Twinkle** (*Terry*). **Doris Day**, 40, made a comeback with *Move Over Darling*, and **Bob Dylan**, a New Yorker, who composed the **Peter, Paul and Mary** hit *Blowin' In The Wind*, had his own concert at London's Festival Hall in May. **The Everly Brothers**, out of the US Marine Corps, got back in the charts with *Ferris Wheel*.

Tragedy struck three times — **Jim Reeves** was killed in a plane crash on July 31, **Johnny Burnette** was drowned on a fishing trip, and **Sam Cooke** was shot dead at a Las Vegas motel.

3

4

5

1

2

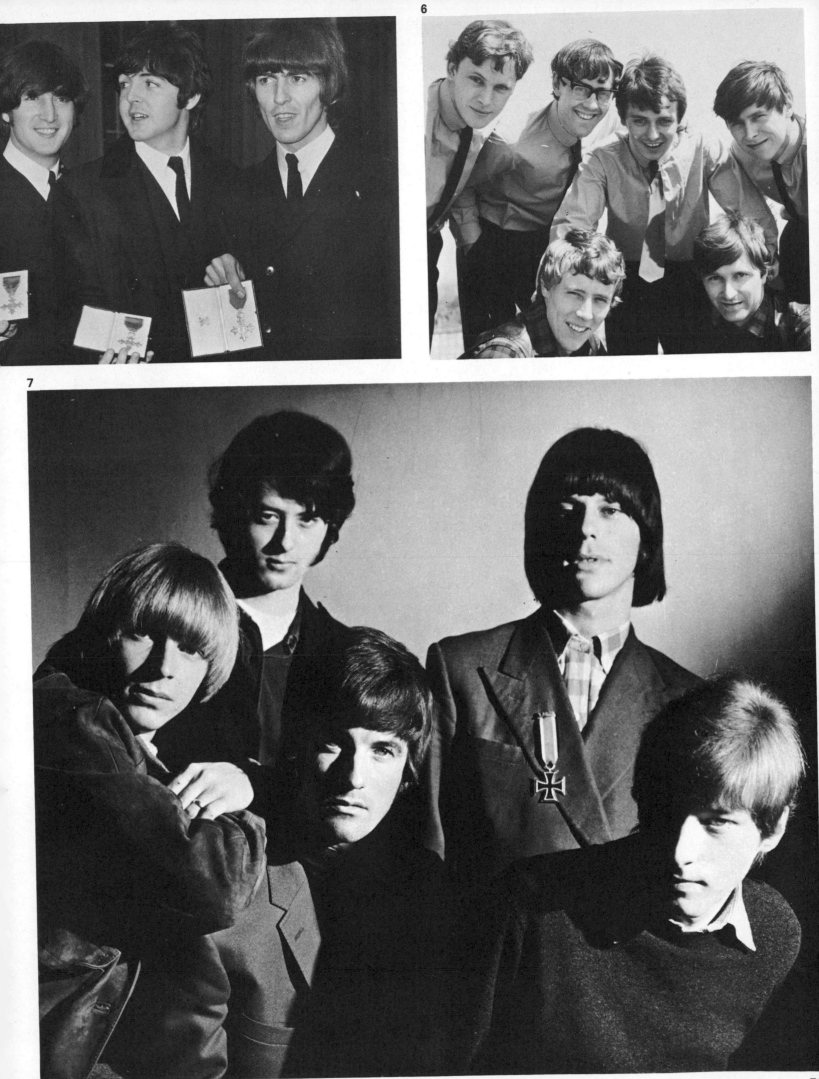

1
Bob Dylan

2
Herman's Hermits

3
Peter and Gordon

4
The Bachelors

5
The Animals

6
Julie Andrews

7
Georgie Fame (centre front)
and the Blue Flames

8
The Supremes

8

1965

This was the year of **The Rolling Stones**. **The Beatles** continued to be the Masters of the group world, but **The Stones** established themselves in the No. 2 world position. They were **Mick Jagger** (lead singer), **Keith Richard** (lead guitar — and composer with Mick), **Bill Wyman** (bass), **Charlie Watts** (drums) and **Brian Jones** (rhythm guitar). The first four are still Stones today, with **Mick Taylor** replacing Brian Jones, who left and soon after was drowned in a swimming pool in 1969.

Their triumphant records of 1965 were *The Last Time*, (I Can't Get No) *Satisfaction* and *Get Off My Cloud*. Their LPs, too, sold by the tens of thousands and everywhere they appeared in person excitement erupted!

The Beatles also had a tremendous year, receiving their MBEs at Buckingham Palace (**Frankie Vaughan** also got an OBE for his Boys' Club work), starring in the biggest pop concert ever given, at Shea's (Baseball) Stadium in New York before 56,000, and meeting **Elvis Presley** at his Bel Air (Hollywood) home.

Their Gold Discs of the year were *Ticket To Ride*, *Eight Days A Week*, *Help*, *Yesterday* (in America **Paul McCartney** alone got the performance credit on the label), *Day Tripper/ We Can Work It Out*, and three LPs — *Beatles VI*, *Help* (film soundtrack), and *Rubber Soul*.

The **Dave Clark Five** continued to surge ahead in America, with Golds for *I Like It Like That*, *Catch Us If You Can* (from a film of same name made in Britain), and *Over And Over*; while **Herman's Hermits**, another teenage rave group in the United States, had no less than six million-sellers in '65 — *Can't You Hear My Heartbeats*, *Silhouettes*, *Mrs Brown You've Got A Lovely Daughter*, *Henery The Eighth I Am*, *Wonderful World* and *Just A Little Bit Better*. Herman and the group also appeared in two Hollywood films, "Where The Boys Meet The Girls" and "Hold On".

Important British newcomers to the million-seller ranks were **Tom Jones** with *It's Not Unusual* (written by his manager Gordon Mills and Les Reed) and *What's New Pussycat*; comedian **Ken Dodd** with *Tears* (he also had *The River* in the British Top Ten), **Wayne Fontana and The Mindbenders** with *Game of Love*; **The Seekers**, an Australian quartet of **Judith Durham** and three male singers, who had three Gold Records for Tom Springfield compositions — *I'll Never Find Another You*, *A World Of Our Own*, and *The Carnival Is Over*; and **The Yardbirds** with *For Your Love* (they are no longer in existence but gave us three famous lead guitarists — **Eric Clapton**, **Jeff Beck** and **Jimmy Page**).

Another Golden act that Britain could claim because they did all their recording in the UK was **The Walker Brothers**, from California and not brothers but **Scott Engel**, **John Maus** and **Gary Leeds**, who all made solo records after splitting. Collectively they were more important, with *Make It Easy On Yourself* their first million-seller.

Two acts to add Golds were **Peter and Gordon** with *True Love Ways*, and **The Kinks** with *Tired Of Waiting For You*.

A lot of other exciting people were happening in Britain in 1965. **The Ivy League** had *Funny How Love Can Be*, and **Billy J. Kramer** had a chart race with **Burt Bacharach** for honours with Burt's *Trains And Boats And Planes*. No. 1 hits included **Cliff Richard's** *The Minute You've Gone*, **Jackie Trent's** *Where Are You Now*, **Sandie Shaw's** *Long Live Love* (one of five hits Sandie had in the year), and **The Hollies'** *I'm Alive*.

Newcomers to the charts included **The Who** (*I Can't Explain*), **Unit 4 + 2** (*Concrete And Clay*), **Donovan** (*Catch The Wind*), **Small Faces** (*Whatcha Gonna Do About It*), **Paul and Barry Ryan**, twin sons of singer **Marion Ryan** (*Don't Bring Me Your Heartaches*), **Spencer Davis** (*Keep On Running*) and **Dave Dee, Dozy, Beaky, Mick and Tich** (*You Make It Move*).

Andy Williams did well with *Almost There* (ironically it stayed at No. 2) and pirate radio from ships off the coast of Britain became popular. Tie-less men's wear came in and much more casual clothes were the order of the day. Sad loss was the death of **Nat 'King' Cole**, and **P. J. Proby** almost ruined his career by splitting his trousers on stage.

And to show how Britain still dominated the American charts, one week their top three in the singles charts read:

1. **Wayne Fontana and The Mindbenders** — *Game Of Love*.
2. **Herman's Hermits** — *Mrs Brown You've Got A Lovely Daughter*.
3. **Freddie and The Dreamers** — *I'm Telling You Now*.

Of course, American artists continued to win more Gold Discs during 1965. **Elvis Presley** was limited to two — *Crying In The Chapel* and *I'm Yours* (from "Tickle Me" film). **Bob Dylan** had two successes: he

Tom Jones had an instant 1965 success with *It's Not Unusual*

2

chanted his own version of *Like A Rolling Stone* to a Gold Disc and watched a new group called **The Byrds** get one of two million-sellers with his *Mr Tambourine Man*, the other with Pete Seeger's *Turn Turn Turn*.

Other Golden newcomers were **The Toys**, a coloured girl trio, with *Lover's Concerto*; **The Four Tops**, still a big attraction, with *I Can't Help Myself*; **Sonny** (Bono) **and Cher** (La Pierre) with *I Got You Babe*; **Sam The Sham and The Pharaohs** *(Wooly Bully)*; **The McCoys** *(Hang On Sloopy)*, **Fontella Bass** *(Rescue Me)*, **Shirley Ellis** *(The Clapping Song)*, **Barry McGuire** *(Eve of Destruction)*, **Len Barry** *(1, 2, 3)* and **Jewel Akens** *(Birds and Bees)*.

The Beach Boys *(Help Me Rhonda)*, **Gene Pitney** *(Looking Thru' The Eyes Of Love)* and **Roger Miller** *(King Of The Road)* added Golds to their collection.

Instrumental successes were the **Ramsey Lewis** (piano, organ) Trio's *The 'In' Crowd*; German pianist **Horst Jankowski's** *A Walk In The Black Forest*; and **Herb Alpert's** *Whipped Cream* LP. The film soundtrack sensation of the year (and years to come) was ''Sound Of Music'' starring (once again!) **Julie Andrews**.

1

3

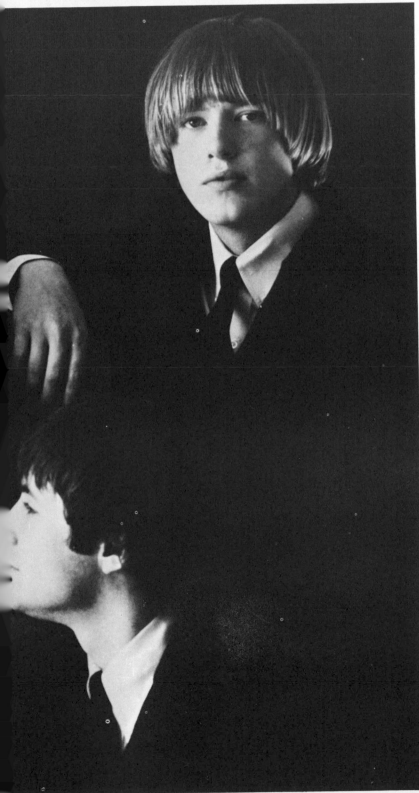

4

5

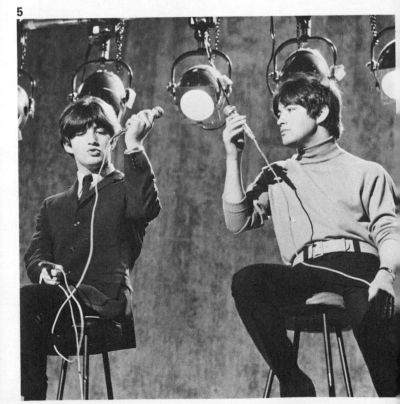

1
Dave Dee, Dozy, Beaky, Mick and Tich

2
The Seekers

3
The Beatles

4
The Small Faces

5
The Rolling Stones

4

1
The Who

2
Procol Harum

88

STEVE MARRIOTT first won fame with Small Faces and now leads the most successful Humble Pie

DAVID BOWIE is one
of Britain's finest
pop showmen as well
as a versatile composer

1966

After the excitement of 1963–4–5, this year was a bit of an anticlimax. **The Beatles** and **The Rolling Stones** were firmly established and nothing as sensational arrived on the scene.

In fact, things went a bit quieter and probably the most important newcomers were three folk-orientated, pleasant-sounding American singing acts — **The Lovin' Spoonful**, a male quartet (*Daydream, Summer In The City*); **The Mamas and The Papas** (two of each) with *California Dreaming* and *Monday Monday*; and (Paul) **Simon** and (Art) **Garfunkel** (singing Paul's compositions, *Sounds of Silence* and *Homeward Bound*). **Bob Dylan** continued to make his presence felt with protest folk songs, earning two more personal Golds with *Rainy Day Woman* and *I Want You*. Britain's answer to Dylan, **Donovan**, came to the fore with his own song, *Sunshine Superman*.

The Beatles kept up their million-sellers with *Paper Back Writer* and a double A-sided single *Yellow Submarine/Eleanor Rigby*, plus several LPs; while **The Stones** added *19th Nervous Breakdown*, *Paint It Black*, and a song that was not so popular, *Have You Seen Your Mother, Baby, Standing In The Shadows*. **The Stones**, after a sensational Albert Hall concert in London, were presented at a party with 20 Gold Discs from various parts of the world.

The Small Faces scored with *Sha-La-La-La-Lee* and *All Or Nothing*, as did **The Walker Brothers** with *The Sun Ain't Gonna Shine Any More*, **Spencer Davis** with *Somebody Help Me*, and **The Who** with *I'm A Boy*. **Dusty Springfield** led a lot of girl singers into the charts with *You Don't Have To Say You Love Me*, and **Tom Jones** won a Gold from *Green Green Grass Of Home*. **Jonathan King**, a brilliant student, won world acclaim for his *Everyone's Gone To The Moon*, and **Manfred Mann's** *Pretty Flamingo* was a big seller.

A new British group, **The Troggs**, had no fewer than three major hits — *Wild Thing*, *With A Girl Like You*, and *I Can't Control Myself*, while other groups in the charts for the first time were **The Overlanders** (*Michelle*), **Los Bravos**, a Spanish group with a German lead singer (*Black Is Black*), **The Temptations** (*Ain't Too Proud To Beg*), **The Sandpipers** (*Guantanamera*) and **The Association** (*Cherish*).

More established groups to win more Golds were **Herman's Hermits** (*A Must To Avoid, You Won't Be Leaving, This Door Swings Both Ways*), **The Kinks** (*Dedicated Followers Of Fashion, Sunny Afternoon*), **The Four Seasons** (*I've Got You Under My Skin*), **The Righteous Brothers** (*Soul And Inspiration*), **The Four Tops** (*Reach Out I'll Be There*), **The Hollies** (*I Can't Let Go, Bus Stop*), **The Animals** (*Inside Looking Out, Don't Bring Me Down*), and **The Beach Boys** (*Barbara Ann/Sloop John B, God Only Knows, Good Vibrations*).

Two novelties to become million-sellers were the **New Vaudeville Band** (making fun of the '30s sound again) with *Winchester Cathedral*; and **Napoleon XIV** with *They're Coming To Take Me Away Ha Haaaaa*. A Vietnam war song, *Ballad of the Green Berets* got S/Sgt **Barry Sadler** a Gold Disc.

Established solo artists to shine in 1966 were **Cliff Richard** with four hits from *Blue Turn To Grey* (by Stones **Mick Jagger** and **Keith Richard**), *Visions, Time Drags By*, and *In The Country*; **The Supremes** with *You Can't Hurry Love*; **The Yardbirds** with *Shape Of Things* and *Over Under Sideways Down*; and **Sonny and Cher** with *What Now My Love*.

Cher had a solo hit with *Bang Bang* and other newcomers with considerable successes were **Lou Christie** (*Lightnin' Strikes*), **Eddy Arnold** (*Make The World Go Away*), **Bert Kaempfert** (*Bye Bye Blues*), **Percy Sledge** (*When A Woman Loves A Man*), **Bobby Hebb** (*Sunny*), **Robert Parker** (*Barefootin'*), **Chris Farlowe** (*Out Of Time*), **Bob Lind** (*Elusive Butterfly*), **Crispian St Peters** (*The Pied Piper*) and Broadway musical star **Barbra Streisand** (*Second Hand Rose*).

The **Sinatras** won two Golds, **Frank** with his swinging *Strangers In The Night* and daughter **Nancy** with *These Boots Were Made For Walking*; while **Elvis Presley** chalked up another three Golds — *Blue River, Frankie and Johnny*, and *Love Letters*. More Golds went to **Stevie Wonder** (*Up Tight*) and the late **Jim Reeves** (*Distant Drums*).

New names to make first appearances in the charts were **Ike and Tina Turner** (*River Deep Mountain High*), **David Garrick** (*Lady Jane*), **Cat Stevens** (*I Love My Dog*), **Easybeats** (*Friday On My Mind*), **Cream** (*Wrapping Paper*), **The Monkees** (*Last Train To Clarksville*) and **Jimmy Ruffin** (*What Becomes Of The Broken*

Simon (right) and Garfunkel

1
Johnny Kidd

2
Troggs

3
Tina Turner

4
Frank and Nancy Sinatra

Hearted).

Tragedy struck twice when **Johnny Kidd** (of Pirates fame) was killed in a car crash, and **Alma Cogan** died after a long fight against cancer.

Groups started to break up — **The Animals** split completely and lead singer **Eric Burdon** reformed **The New Animals**, while organist **Alan Price** formed his own **Set** *(I Put A Spell On You)*, and bassist **Chas Chandler** became manager of an American guitarist called **Jimi Hendrix**. Drummer **Chris Curtis** left **The Searchers**, Stevie **Winwood** quit **Spencer Davis**, vocalist **Mike d'Abo** joined **Manfred Mann** when singer **Paul Jones** left and got a solo hit with *High Time*.

Finally, **Paul McCartney** grew a moustache — the first of the hairy **Beatles** to come.

1

2

3

1

1
Jimmy Ruffin

2
Easy Beats

3
Cat Stevens

4
Cream

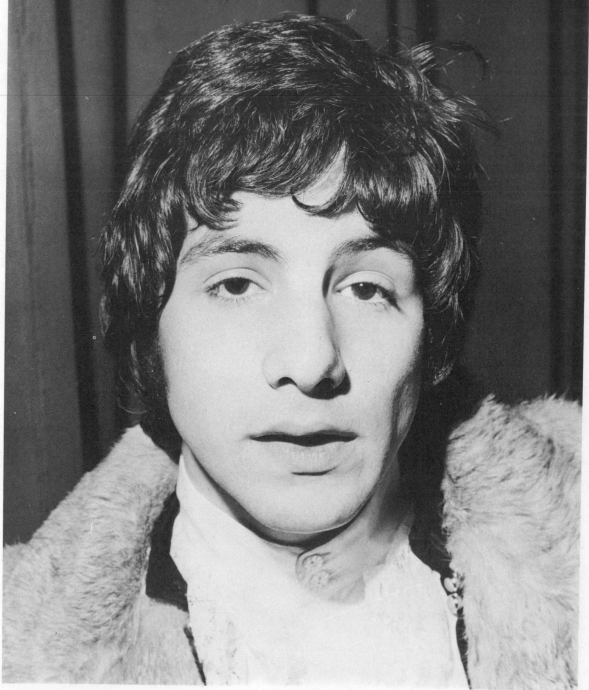

1967

The **Monkees** made up the most remarkable group of the year, with four Gold Discs and winning millions of fans between the age of 5 and 15. They were a prefabricated pop group. First scripts were written for a mad-mad TV series in which four young fellows did crazy things to help people in need or get jobs for their pop group. From hundreds of auditions **Peter Tork**, a folk singer, **Mike Nesmith**, a country-jazz singer-guitarist, **Micky Dolenz**, formerly in "Circus Boy" children's TV series and a drummer, and **Davy Jones**, an English youngster who was in the musical "Mr Pickwick", were chosen.

First class songwriters were enlisted to write for them and the group's multi-million-sellers were *Last Train To Clarksville*, *I'm A Believer*, *Little Bit Me Little Bit You*, and *Pleasant Valley Sunday*. They came to Britain for five packed shows at Wembley Pool, playing, as in America, mostly to children between 5 and 15. Record sales soared with this age group and their TV series was watched by millions.

But **The Monkees** threw it all away by internal fights and antagonising their young fans by denying they were teenybop idols but serious musicians. Strangely enough, no other group or young star cashed in on **The Monkees'** popularity, unlike today with **David Cassidy**, **The Osmonds** and **The Jackson Five** and other groups and singers exciting the very young record buyers.

While the weenyboppers were kept happy by **The Monkees**, a big change was happening in **The Beatles'** camp. After single Golds from *Penny Lane/Strawberry Fields* (Liverpool place names), and *All You Need Is Love*, they brought out an album called *Sergeant Pepper's Lonely Hearts Club Band*, which was much more intricate musically and had lyrics which took a lot of thinking about, some with drug connotations, a far cry from their earlier tunes. It was the start of the underground, psychadelic music era to come.

Other underground pioneer groups made the British charts as early as 1967, including **Pink Floyd** with *Arnold Layne*, **The Doors** with *Light My Fire*, and **The Move**, who broke things up on stage, with *Night Of Fear* and then *Flowers In The Rain* (part of their publicity was a cartoon featuring Prime Minister Harold Wilson which brought a libel action and resulted in most of the royalties of the song going to charity!). Three other records with more sophisticated music were *Hey Joe*, by **The Jimi Hendrix Experience**, *Hi Ho Silver Lining* by ex-Yardbird guitarist **Jeff Beck**, and *Paper Sun* by **Traffic**, which featured **Steve Winwood**. And to add momentum to the heavier music, **The Beatles** took their weirdo film trip in a coach for their "Magical Mystery Tour" film.

But simpler, more tuneful music was still much in demand and no fewer than three Gold Discs went to **The Tremeloes** (now without **Brian Poole**) for *Here Comes My Baby*, *Silence Is Golden*, and *Even The Bad Times Are Good*; **Herman's Hermits** for *There's A Kind Of Hush*, **Spencer Davis** group for *Gimme Some Lovin'*, **Hollies** (*On A Carousel*, and *Carrie Anne*), **Procol Harum** (*Whiter Shade Of Pale*), three young fellows from Australia, **The Bee Gees** (*Massachusetts*, after a first hit with *New York Mining Disaster*), and **Foundations** (*Baby Now That I've Found You*).

Engelbert Humperdinck had his best year ever with *Release Me*, *There Goes My Everything* and *The Last Waltz* winning him three Golds. **Donovan** had a million-seller with *Mellow Yellow* and **The Seekers** with *Georgy Girl*, **Petula Clark** with *This Is My Song* and **Sandie Shaw** with *Puppet On A String*, the Bill Martin-Phil Coulter song which won the Eurovision Song Festival for Britain for the very first time.

Lulu topped the American charts with *To Sir With Love*, the title of the film she played in with Sidney Poitier, and **Long John Baldry** won a Gold with *Let The Heartaches Begin*, as did **Whistling Jack Smith** with *I Was Kaiser Bill's Batman*.

All these were British million-sellers, matched by Americans such as **The Supremes** with three Golds — *You Keep Me Hanging On*, *The Happening* and *Reflections*; **The Four Tops** (*Standing In The Shadow Of Love*), **Mamas and Papas** (*Dedicated To The One I Love*), **Turtles** (*Happy Together* and *She'd Rather Be With Me*), **Aretha Franklin** (*Respect*), **Association** (*Windy*, and *Never My Love*), **Vikki Carr** (*It Must Be Him*), **Stevie Wonder** (*I Was Made To Love Her*), **Frankie Valli**, of Four Seasons fame (*Can't Take My Eyes Off You*) and **Bobby Vee** (*Come Back When You Grow Up*).

Notable newcomers with first Golds were **The Royal Guardsmen** (*Snoopy v. The Red Baron*), **The Buckinghams** (*Kind Of A Drag*), **Arthur Conley** (*Sweet Soul Music*), **The Happenings** (*I Got Rhythm*), **Bobbie Gentry** (*Ode To Billie Joe*), comedian **Bill Cosby**

Engelbert Humperdinck won three Gold Discs in 1967

(Little Ole Man) and **The Box Tops** *(The Letter)*.

In Britain, **Paul Jones** made a solo hit with *I'm A Bad Bad Boy* from his starring film "Privilege", a startling futuristic look at pop in the next century; pirate radio was killed by Parliament and BBC Radio 1 took its place with jingles and many of its deejays; and the **Walker Brothers** broke up a wealthy association. In America **Elvis Presley** got married to Priscilla Beaulieu; and **Bob Dylan** was badly injured in a motor bike crash and took a long lay-off.

New names came into the British charts, including **Gladys Knight and The Pips** *(Take Me In Your Arms Again)*, Israeli actor **Topol** *(If I Was a Rich Man)*, Tamla's **Marvin Gaye and Kim Weston** *(It Takes Two)*, **The Dubliners** *(Seven Drunken Nights)*, **P.P.** (Pat) **Arnold** *(First Cut Is The Deepest)*, **The Johnny Mann Singers** *(Up Up And Away*, a song by Jim Webb*)* reggae singer **Desmond Dekker** *(007)*, **Anita Harris** *(Just Lovin' You)*, **Amen Corner** *(Gin House)*, **Keith West** (Excerpt from "Teenage Opera", first of pop-rock operas), **The Herd** *(From The Underground)*, **Des O'Connor** *(Careless Hands)*, **Sam and Dave** *(Soul Man)* and a Liverpool satirical group called **The Scaffold**, featuring **Mike McGear**, Paul McCartney's brother, singing *Thank You Very Much*, which left the nation wondering what the Aintree Iron was . . . and what was it, anyway?

And **Frank Sinatra** teamed up with daughter **Nancy** to get a No. 1 in Britain with *Somethin' Stupid*.

The **Beatles'** manager, Brian Epstein, died suddenly at the age of 32 and the group's affairs were thrown into a turmoil they have never quite recovered from (the start of the end of the **Beatles**), and rhythm-and-blues singer **Otis Redding**, 26, was killed in an air crash.

5

Vic Lewis presents the
MONKEES
...T WEMBLEY
...ay June...
...turday Ju...
...nday Jul...

6

1
Aretha Franklin

2
Anita Harris

3
The Move

1
Robin, Maurice and Barry
Gibb – The Bee Gees

2
Pink Floyd

1

2

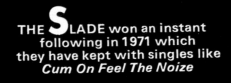

THE **S**LADE won an instant
following in 1971 which
they have kept with singles like
Cum On Feel The Noize

MICHAEL JACKSON the dynamic lead singer of the famous Tamla teenbop group, the Jackson Five

1
Jeff Beck

2
Jim Morrison, of The Doors

3
Traffic

109

1968

The **Beatles** were a confused group in 1968 — and so were their followers. They didn't seem to know what they wanted to do or which way their careers should go. So they went to India to study meditation under a guru called Maharishi Mahesh Yogi. They wrote some good tunes there, although they admitted they weren't very good converts. They soon became disillusioned, specially when the Maharishi is alleged to have sold the rights to film the Beatles and himself to an American company, without asking the Beatles. And later the guru went on tour with the **Beach Boys** in America and it proved a complete disaster.

There is no doubt **The Beatles** still had a big following, although not nearly as large as in the early days when they kept their music simple. They had three million-selling singles — *Hello Goodbye, Hey Jude* and *Lady Madonna*. And their LPs sold well — *Sgt Pepper, Magical Mystery Tour* and their first double-album of 30 tracks, costing £3.70, which still topped the LP charts and even got into the singles sales list for selling more than some singles — a million-seller that made many millions!

The Beatles also sponsored a young Welsh lady who won a Gold Disc for her first record, **Mary Hopkin** with *Those Were The Days*, produced by **Paul McCartney**. And they were behind **The Grapefruit**, who had a hit with *Dear Delilah*.

The Rolling Stones had two more Golds from *Jumping Jack Flash* and *Street Fighting Man*, and produced some weird music on *Their Satanic Majesties Request* LP, which sold well but not as well as former LPs.

Solo singers **Tom Jones** and **Engelbert Humperdinck** sold in their millions, due to their great success in America, where they played the best night clubs and stadiums. **Elvis Presley** was at the first night of Tom's Flamingo, Las Vegas, engagement. Tom's 1968 hits were *Help Yourself* and *Delilah*, and Engelbert's *Am I That Easy To Forget, A Man Without Love* and *Bicyclettes de Belsize*.

Underground music gained ground, specially in the LP market, which started to become more important than singles to the retailers, and some underground groups refused to make singles, saying they couldn't get their message over in less than three minutes.

More pop stars were given major TV series of their own, including **Tom Jones, Engelbert Humperdinck, Sandie Shaw, Cilla Black, Lulu, Dusty Springfield,** folk singer **Julie Felix** and **Val Doonican**. They sold more records as a consequence.

Pop music tastes varied more than ever which led to many more No. 1 hits staying less weeks in the charts and more newcomers to the best selling lists. The important Gold Disc winners were **Donovan** with *Jennifer Juniper* and *Hurdy Gurdy Man*, Continental orchestra leader **Paul Mauriat's** *Love Is Blue*, **Simon and Garfunkel's** *Mrs Robinson* (from "The Graduate" film), **Marvin Gaye's** *I Heard It Through The Grapevine*, **Herb Alpert's** *This Guy's In Love With You*, **The Doors'** *Hello I Love You* (Won't You Tell Me Your Name), **The (Young) Rascals'** *People Got To Be Free* and *A Beautiful Morning*, **Jeannie C. Riley's** *Harper Valley P.T.A.*, the late **Otis Redding's** *Dock On The Bay* (he also won several Golds for LPs after his death, just as **Jim Reeves** did before him), and **Diana Ross** (she got solo billing now) **and The Supreme's** *Love Child*.

Newcomers to sell a million were **Steppenwolf**, a group originating in Toronto, Canada *(Born To Be Wild)*, **Strawberry Alarm Clock** *(Incense And Peppermints)*, **John Fred and The Playboys** *(Judy In Disguise)*, **Lemon Pipers** *(Green Tambourine)*, **Bobby Goldsboro** *(Honey)*, **Archie Bell and The Drells** *(Tighten Up)*, **Hugh Maskela** *(Grazin' In The Grass)*, **Georgie Fame** *(Ballad Of Bonnie And Clyde)*, **Manfred Mann** *(The Mighty Quinn)*, **Gary Puckett and The Union Gap** *(Young Girl)*, **Tommy James and The Shondells** *(Mony Mony)*, **Joe Cocker** *(With A Little Help From My Friends)*, **Ohio Express** *(Yummy Yummy Yummy)*, **O. C. Smith** *(Little Green Apples)*, **Box Tops** *(Cry Like A Baby)*, **1910 Fruitgum Company** *(Simon Says)*, **American Breed** *(Bend Me Shape Me)*. And **The Monkees** were still around with a Gold from *Valleri*.

Cliff Richard got to No. 1 spot again in the British charts with *Congratulations*, consolation for coming second with this song in the 1968 Eurovision Song Contest. Among other British No. 1s were **The Love Affair** with *Everlasting Love*, **Esther and Abi Ofarim** *(Cinderella Rockafella)*, **Louis Armstrong** *(What A Wonderful World)*, **The Equals** *(Baby Come Back)*, **The Bee Gees** *(I've Got To Get A Message To You)*, orchestra leader **Hugo Montenegro** *(The Good The Bad And The Ugly* — film theme), **Barry Ryan**, solo now *(Eloise)* and **The Scaffold** *(Lily The Pink)*.

There were many newcomers to the American and British charts dur-

Mary Hopkin's first success was in 1968

1
O. C. Smith

2
Julie Driscoll and the Brian
Auger Trinity

3
Joe Cocker

ing the year, including **Plastic Penny** (Everything I Am), **Solomon King** (She Wears My Ring), **Status Quo** (Pictures Of Matchstick Men), one-man-band **Don Partridge** (Rosie), two new singers, **John Rowles** (If I Only Had Time) and **Malcolm Roberts** (May I Have The Next Dream With You), **The Paper Dolls** (Something Here In My Heart), **The Honeybus** (I Can't Let Maggie Go), **Jacky** (White Horses), **Julie Driscoll** and **Brian Augur Trinity** (This Wheel's On Fire), **Marmalade** (Lovin' Things), **O. C. Smith** (Son Of Hickory Holler's Tramp), **Richard Harris**, the actor (McArthur Park), **Crazy World Of Arthur Brown** (Fire), **Sly and The Family Stone** (Dance To The Music), **Canned Heat** (On The Road Again), **Johnny Nash** (Hold Me Tight), **Casuals** (Jesamine), **Leapy Lee** (Little Arrows), **Mason Williams** (Classical Gas), **Fleetwood Mac** (Need Your Love So Bad), **The Band**, ex-Bob Dylan backing group (The Weight), **Jose Feliciano** (Light My Fire), **Bonzo Dog Doo Dah Band** (I'm The Urban Spaceman), **Kasenetz Katz Singing Orchestral Circus**, 8 Buddah label groups combined (Quick Joey Small) and from Greece **Aphrodites Child** (Rain And Tears).

Well known names that came back to the charts were headed by **Elvis Presley**, who, after Indescribably Blue in March 1967, had been missing for a whole year, then came back in March, 1968, with Guitar Man. **Cilla Black** was back with Step Inside Love and **Andy Williams** with Can't Take My Eyes Off You. **The Small Faces** had two more with Tin Soldier and Lazy Sunday, **The Move** with Fire Brigade, and **Dave Dee** with Xanadu. **The Dave Clark Five** came back with Red Balloon, and **Mama Cass** went solo with Dream A Little Dream Of Me, while **Ray Charles** did the Beatles's Eleanor Rigby.

Four British acts to have hits in America and not in Britain (until later) were **Cream** (White Room), **Deep Purple** (Hush), **Don Fardon** (Indian Reservation) and **Eric Burdon and The** (new) **Animals** (Monterey). Other new names to come on the scene were **The Fifth Dimension**, a coloured vocal quintette (Stoned Soul Picnic, and Sweet Blindness), pianist **Sergio Mendez and Brazil '66** (The Fool On The Hill), **Creedence Clearwater Revival** (Suzie Q), and **The Cowsills** (We Can Fly).

More established recording artists had more hits — **The Tremeloes** with Helule Helule and My Little Lady; **Des O'Connor** with I Pretend and One Two Three O'Leary; **The Who** with Dogs, and Magic Bus; **Moody Blues** with Voices In The Sky; **Beach Boys** with Do It Again; **The Turtles** with Elenore; **The Foundations** with Build Me Up Buttercup; and **Dusty Springfield** with I Close My Eyes And Count To Ten.

Finally, LPs that were constantly in the charts in 1968 were those of **The Beatles**, **Rolling Stones**, **Val Doonican**, **Tom Jones**, **Monkees**, **Traffic**, **Beach Boys**, **Bob Dylan's** John Wesley Harding, **Supremes**, **Cream**, **Hollies**, **Jethro Tull**, **Moody Blues**, **Pink Floyd**, "Sound Of Music" film soundtrack, **Mantovani**, **Simon and Garfunkel**, **Engelbert Humperdinck**, **Jimi Hendrix Experience**, **Scott Walker**, **Bert Kaemphert**, **Incredible String Band**, **Small Faces**, **Cilla Black**, **Donovan**, **Move**, the late **Otis Redding**, and many, many more.

1

2

1
Keith Richard and Mick
Jagger of The Rolling Stones

2
Bobby Goldsboro

3
Esther and Abi Ofarim

4
Gary Puckett and the
Union Gap

1

2

3

1969

The LP really broke through and became more important than the single during this year. Of 158 recordings awarded Gold Discs, 96 were LPs and 62 singles. A new pop sensation was badly needed, but it failed to turn up. Underground, or heavy, music groups increased, some created from the breaking up of other groups. And some of Britain's best groups almost lived in America, where they could get more money from one large concert than from an entire tour in the UK.

Solo singers did well, especially from LP sales. **Tom Jones** had no less than five Gold-winning LPs during 1969, matched only by country singer **Glen Campbell** (who shared one with **Bobbie Gentry**). **Elvis Presley** had three, and those with two each were **The Beatles**, **The Rolling Stones**, **Engelbert Humperdinck**, **Dean Martin**, **Judy Collins**, **Johnny Cash** and **Led Zeppelin**, a British group very popular in America. Two notable albums were **The Who's** pop opera *Tommy*, and the return of **Bob Dylan** after his motor cycle accident, with *Nashville Skyline*.

Several groups known more for LPs than singles and who had Golds in 1969 were **The Brooklyn Bridge**, **Cream**, **Iron Butterfly**, **Crosby Stills and Nash**, **The Jimi Hendrix Experience**, **Santana**, **Janis Joplin**, **Chicago Transit Authority**, **Three Dog Night** and **Blind Faith**.

Groups which had both single (named here) and LP Golds were **The Beatles** (*Get Back*, *Something*, *Ballad Of John And Yoko*), **Rolling Stones** (*Honky Tonk Woman*), **Doors** (*Touch Me*), **Sly and The Family Stone** (*Everyday People*), **Steppenwolf** (*Magic Carpet Ride*), **1910 Fruitgum Company** (*Indian Giver*), **Isley Brothers** (*It's Your Thing*), **Cowsills** (*Hair*), **Fifth Dimension** (*Aquarius/Let The Sunshine In*, and *Wedding Bell Blues*), **Edwin Hawkins Singers** (*Oh Happy Day*), **Blood Sweat and Tears** (*You Make Me So Very Happy*, and *Spinning Wheel*), **Henry Mancini** (Love Theme from "Romeo and Juliet" film), **Peter, Paul and Mary** (*Jet Plane*), **The Guess Who**, a Canadian group (*Those Eyes* and *Laughing*), **Three Dog Night** (*One*), **The Archies**, a mythical group featured in a TV cartoon film (*Sugar Sugar*), **Zager and Evans** (*In The Year 2525*) and **Ohio Express** (*Chewy Chewy*).

Newcomers to the Gold Record ranks with singles were **Jackie de Shannon** (*Put A Little Love In Your Heart*), **Neil Diamond** (*Holly Holly*, and *Sweet Caroline*), **Tyrone Davis** (*Can I Change My Mind*), **B. J. Thomas** (*Hooked On A Feeling*, and *Oh My Head*), **Jerry Butler** (*Only The Strong Survive*), the British group **The Zombies** (*Time Of The Season*), **Joe Simon** (*The Chokin' Kind*), **Oliver** (*Jean*), **Andy Kim** (*Baby I Love You*), **R. B. Greaves** (*Take A Letter To Maria*) and a teenagers' rave, **Bobby Sherman** (*Little Woman*). Adding to their Golds were **Dion** (*Abraham Martin And John*), **Aretha Franklin** (*See Saw*), **Glen Campbell** (*Witchita Linesman*, and *Galveston*), **Tommy Roe** (*Dizzy, Sheila, and Sweet Pea*), **Tom Jones** (*I'll Never Fall In Love Again*), **Ray Stevens** (*Gitarzan*) and **Johnny Cash** (*A Boy Named Sue*).

In the British charts there were some new names at the top. **Marmalade**, a Scottish group, got to No. 1 with *Ob La Di Ob La Da*, a Beatles song; **Fleetwood Mac** with *Albatross* and later *Oh Well*; **The Move** with *Blackberry Way*; **Amen Corner** with *Half As Nice*; **Peter Sarstedt**, brother of Eden Kane, with *Where Do You Go To*; **Thunderclap Newman** with *Something In The Air*; **John Lennon's Plastic Ono Band** with *Give Peace A Chance*; and for the 15th time in 12 years, **Elvis Presley** with *In The Ghetto*; **Creedence Clearwater Revival** with *Bad Moon Rising*; **Bobbie Gentry** with *I'll Never Fall In Love Again*; **Stevie Wonder** with *Yester-Me, Yester-You, Yesterday*; **Kenny Rogers and The First Edition** with *Ruby Don't Take Your Love To Town*; and **Blue Mink** with *Melting Pot*, plus **The Beatles** twice, **Tommy Roe** and **Zager and Evans**.

New names to the charts which went on to greater things were **Jethro Tull**, a group headed by **Ian Anderson**, with *Love Story*, and *Sweet Dreams*; **Clodagh Rodgers** with *Come Back And Shake Me*; **Chicken Shack** with *I'd Rather Go Blind*; **Family Dogg** with *Way Of Life*; **David Bowie** (*Space Oddity*); **Nilsson** (*Everybody's Talking*); **Joe Dolan** (*Make Me An Island*); **Robin Gibb**, solo after leaving Bee Gees, to which he returned later (*Something In The Air*); organist **Johnny Preston** (*That's The Way God Planned It*); **Humble Pie** (*Natural Born Bugie*); **Fairport Convention** (*Si Tu Dois Partir*); **The Peddlers** (*Birth*) and **The Family** (*No Mule's Fool*). Old-timers to re-appear were **Frank Sinatra** (*Love's Been Good To Me*) and **Donald Peers** (*Please Don't Go*).

Reggae was becoming popular through hit discs from **Max Romeo** (*Wet Dream*), **The Upsetters** (*Return To Django*), **Harry J. All-**

Judy Collins had two very successful LPs in 1969

stars *(The Liquidators)*, **Jimmy Cliff** *(Wonderful World Beautiful People)*, and **The Pioneers** *(Long Shot Kick The Bucket)*.

Among the group casualties were **The Shadows**, who broke up after ten years, **The Jimi Hendrix Experience**, **The Hollies** who lost **Graham Nash** to **Crosby Stills and Nash**. Peter Frampton left **The Herd** and **Stevie Marriott** the **Faces** to form **Humble Pie**, **Cream** and **Traffic** broke up and **Blind Faith** was created, **The Move** had changes, and **Manfred Mann** broke up.

There were two free concerts in London's Hyde Park, with 120,000 attending **Blind Faith's** show and 250,000 going to see **The Rolling Stones**, who later played to 500,000 in California. **John Lennon** divorced his first wife Cynthia and married **Yoko Ono** and they started the **Plastic Ono Band** together, **Paul McCartney** married Linda Eastman, **Lulu** married Bee Gee **Maurice Gibb**, and **Cilla Black** married her manager Bobby Willis. **Mick Jagger** was "Ned Kelly" in the film of that name and **Ringo Starr** joined Peter Sellers in "The Magic Christian". And the tragedy of the year was the death by drowning in a swimming pool of ex-Rolling Stone **Brian Jones**.

20

3

4

5

6

1
Zager and Evans

2
Chicago

3
Crosby, Stills and Nash
(from left, Nash, Stills and
Crosby)

1

2

3

1
Jethro Tull

2
Guess Who

DAVID CASSIDY became world
famous as a member of the
television Partridge Family,
later establishing himself
as a top recording star

MARC BOLAN has topped
the charts many times
with his T. Rex group

1
Glen Campbell

2
Janis Joplin

1970

Pop music moved into the '70s in a rather uncertain way. There was still no new sensation, no real leader. Record buyers followed a wide variety of tastes, as shown by the great number of newcomers to the scene and the quick-changing hit parade. **The Beatles** were definitely on the break-up. Marriage was partly the reason, because John and Yoko Lennon turned more and more to doing their own thing, and Paul and Linda McCartney did the same. Furthermore, there was a disagreement over management. John, George and Ringo favouring Allen Klein, a New York businessman, as their financial manager, and Paul McCartney appointing Lee Eastman, his father-in-law. **The Beatles** were still linked by Apple Records, which they had instigated towards the end of their recording together, and by Northern Songs, their publishers, but John and Paul stopped writing together.

Nevertheless, in the million-selling lists of 1970 were **Beatles** single and LP of *Let It Be*, and their *Hey Jude* LP. Other Gold Discs were won for individual effort – the **Plastic Ono Band's** *Live – Peace In Toronto* LP, the McCartney LP, John and Yoko's *Instant Karma* single, and **George Harrison's** *My Sweet Lord* single and *All Things Must Pass* LP, while Ringo made two fairly successful LPs – *Sentimental Journey* and *Beaucoup of Blues*. He continued filming and appeared in the top American comedy show "Laugh In".

A far more successful group in 1970 was California's **Creedence Clearwater Revival**, led by multi-instrumentalist-composer **John Fogarty**. The foursome had five singles – *Down On The Corner, Travelin' Band, Bad Moon Rising, Up Around The Bend* and *Looking Out The Backdoor* – and six LPS, including their *Cosmo's Factory*, awarded Gold Records during the year.

Britain's **Moody Blues** had a very good year too, with no less than five LPs declared million-sellers, including *A Question Of Balance* and *Our Children's Children's Children*; and **Joe Cocker** had three Golds for LPs, including his *With A Little Help From My Friends*.

Other British million-seller successes were **Tom Jones** *(Without Love* and an album), **Engelbert Humperdinck** (three LPs), **Mungo Jerry** *(In The Summertime* single, which sold over three million copies), **Edison Lighthouse** *(Love Grows)*, **Donovan** *(A Gift From A Flower To A Garden* LP*)*, **Vanity Fair** *(Hitchin' A Ride)*, **Free** *(Alright Now)* and albums by **The Who** *(Live At Leeds)*, **Led Zeppelin**, **Jethro Tull** and **Traffic**.

Britain was still getting its fair share of the LP hits in America. On February 21, the American LP chart read: 1. **Led Zeppelin**; 2. *Abbey Road* – **Beatles**; 4. **Tom Jones'** *Live In Las Vegas*; 6. *Let It Bleed* – **Rolling Stones**; 7. **Engelbert Humperdink**; and 10. **Joe Cocker** – six out of ten!

Simon and Garfunkel achieved a remarkable feat, with their single and LP of *Bridge Over Troubled Waters* being No. 1 in both the LP and single charts of both America and Britain at the same time. They also had a big hit with *Cecilia*.

The film version of the Woodstock pop festival in America did record business and Britain's three-day Isle of Wight festival in September drew a crowd of some 100,000 and stars from all of the world, including **Chicago, Family, Procol Harum, Joni Mitchell, Emerson Lake and Palmer, Who, Free, Doors, Ten Years After, John Sebastian, Mungo Jerry, Sly and The Family Stone, Jethro Tull, Jimi Hendrix, Joan Baez, Richie Havens, Leonard Cohen, Moody Blues, Donovan** and a crazy falsetto singer called **Tiny Tim**. And an extensive European tour was taken by **The Rolling Stones**, who had another Gold for their *Get Yer Ya Ya's Out* album.

Tom Jones and **Cliff Richard** had a major TV series each (and Cliff had his 50th chart hit, eight being No. 1s), **Cilla Black** became a mother and **Dana** *(All Kinds Of Everything)* of Eire put **Mary Hopkin** *(Knock Knock)* into second place in the Eurovision Song Contest.

Underground groups continued to win fame and reach the overground, although many broke up and formed new ones. Among the Gold Disc winners were albums from **Jefferson Airplane** (two), **Doors** (two), **Steppenwolf** (two), **Blood Sweat and Tears, Grass Roots, Three Dog Night** (two), **Grand Funk Railroad** (three), **The Band, Santana, Sly and The Family Stone, Mountain** and **Chicago**.

Elvis Presley kept prominent with *Suspicious Minds, Don't Cry Daddy* and *The Wonder Of You*, and an LP – *From Elvis To Memphis*; and **Bob Dylan** had three Golds from *Self Portrait, New Morning* and *Freewheelin'* albums. **The Fifth Dimension** had a good year, with three Golden LPs and a big single *One Less Bell To Answer*. **Peter, Paul and Mary** had three Gold LPs and **The Lettermen** and **The**

Paul McCartney formed Wings after the break-up of The Beatles in 1970

Carpenters also had Golds. **Jose Feliciano** had two more million-selling albums as well, and **James Taylor** made his Gold debut with *Sweet Baby James*.

The progressive vocal group **Crosby, Stills, Nash** had added **'and (Neil) Young'**, gaining a hit with their *Deja Vu* LP and being connected with two solo LPs by **Neil Young** and two by **Steve Stills** (one with **Bloomfield and Kooper**).

On the more conventional vocal side, **Frank Sinatra** and **Dionne Warwick** had two Gold LPs each and **Andy Williams**, **Glen Campbell**, **Neil Diamond**, **Joni Mitchell**, **Dean Martin**, **Judy Collins** and the team of **Nancy Sinatra** and **Lee Hazelwood** had one each.

Canada was prominent in 1970, the Maple Music sound beginning to win over America and Britain via Golds for **The Guess Who** (two LPs and a massive single called *American·Woman*), **Anne Murray** *(Snowbird)* and **The Poppy Family** *(Which Way You Goin Billy)*.

The weenybop front was most active, with **The Jackson Five** starting to become a force. This Motown group of young American coloured boys, aged from 10 to 18, had *I Want You Back*, *The Love You Save*, *ABC* and *I'll Be There* singles and three No. 1 LPs in America, with their *Diana Ross Introduces The Jackson Five* album selling two million copies in three months! This group, young though it is, sings very good rhythm-and-blues, apart from being a big weenybop attraction. The **Partridge Family**, an American TV series for children and from whence came teen idol **David Cassidy**, had a big single with *I Think I Love You* and a million-selling LP, while **The Archies**, **Bobby Sherman** (three Gold LPs) and **Mark Lindsay** all kept the very young happy.

Country-and-Western had several million selling LPs, among them *The Best of* **Charley Pride** (he was unusual in that he became a top country singer despite being coloured). *Hello I'm* **Johnny Cash**, **Loretta Lynn's** *Don't Come Home A'Drinkin'*, **Tammy's (Wynette)** *Greatest Hits*, **Merle Haggard's** *Oki From Muskogee*, and **Jim Nabors'** *Christmas Album*.

Million-selling soundtracks were "Easy Rider", "Woodstock", "Midnight Cowboy", "Paint Your Wagon", "Jimi Hendrix/Otis Redding At Monterey" and two years before the stage version various artists sang the hit songs from "Jesus Christ Superstar" and won a Gold.

Instrumental Golds included **Jimi Hendrix's** *Band of Gypsies*, **Herb Alpert's** *Warm*, **Mantovani's** *Golden Hits* and a trio of Golds for **Burt Bacharach** – *Butch Cassidy and The Sundance Kid*, *Make It Easy On Yourself*, and *Reach Out*.

Some of the big single songs of 1970, not yet mentioned, were *Everything Is Beautiful* **(Ray Stevens)**, *Raindrops Are Falling On My Head* **(B. J. Thomas** in America, **Sacha Distel** in Europe), *Long and Winding Road* **(Beatles)**, *Mama Told Me Not To Come* **(Three Dog Night)**, *Balls of Confusion* **(Temptations)**, *Close To You* and *We've Only Just Begun* **(Carpenters)**, *Spill The Wine* **(Eric Burdon and War** – combinations of English star and American coloured group), *Venus* **(Shocking Blue**, a Dutch group), *War* **(Edwin Starr)**, *Ain't No Mountain High Enough* **(Diana Ross and Supremes)**, *Candida* **(Dawn)**, *Cracklin' Rosie* **(Neil Diamond)**, *Tears Of A Clown* **(Smokey Robinson and Miracles)**, *Ride A White Swan* **(T Rex)**, *It's All In The Game* **(Four Tops)**, *Yellow River*, and *San Barnadino* **(Christie)**, *Whole Lotta Love* **(CCS** – an Alixis Korner group).

Others were *Band of Gold* **(Freda Payne)**, *Spirit In The Sky* **(Norman Greenbaum)**, *Something* **(Shirley Bassey)**, *Wandering Star* **(Lee Marvin)**, *Groovin With Mr Bloe* (Mr Bloe – **Zack Lawrence**), *Can't Help Falling In Love* **(Andy Williams)**, *Back Home* **(England's World Cup Squad)**, *Two Little Boys* **(Rolf Harris)**, *Lola* **(Kinks)**, *Black Night* **(Deep Purple)**, *Honey Come Back* **(Glen Campbell)**, *Cotton Fields* **(Beach Boys)**, *Woodstock* **(Matthews Southern Comfort)**, *Goodbye Sam Hello Samantha* **(Cliff Richard)**, and *Voodoo Chile* **(Jimi Hendrix)**.

There were literally dozens of newcomers to the British charts in 1970, notably **White Plains**, **Juicy Lucy**, **Frijid Pink**, **Richard Barnes**, **Gerry Monroe** (with **Gracie Fields'** *Sally*!), **Tony Joe White**, **Badfinger**, **Pickettywitch**, **Hot Chocolate**, **Chairmen of the Board**, **Dave Edmunds**, **McGuinness Flint**, **Gilbert O'Sullivan** and Reggae's **Byron Lee**, **Bob and Marcia** and **Horace Faith**.

Finally, two interesting titles, both selling over a million discs – *Groove Didn't I* (Blow Your Mind This Time), jargon of the progressive era, by **The Delfonics**, and *Thank You* (Falettinme Be Mice Elf Again), the mis-spelt title fad, by **Sly and The Family Stone**.

Tragedy struck four times with the untimely deaths of Motown singer **Tammi Terrell** (24), **Canned Heat's Al Wilson** (23), **Jimi Hendrix** (24), and **Janis Joplin** (25), a hell-raising rock singer.

1
Sacha Distel

2
Alexis Korner

3
Gilbert O'Sullivan

4
Christie

5
Canned Heat

6
The Partridge Family

4

5

6

1
Freda Payne

2
James Taylor

3
Anne Murray

4
Led Zeppelin

1971

Britain produced some very valuable disc newcomers during this year, who won international fame in the heavy and lighter pop fields. In the former were **Elton John**, a pianist-vocalist-composer with a flare for flamboyant showmanship; **Rod Stewart**, a singer with a distinctive, husky voice, backed by **The Faces** group most of the time; **Black Sabbath**, a progressive rock group; and three very fine rock musicians — **Emerson, Lake and Palmer**.

And on the lighter side, also selling records by the million, were **The Slade**, a Wolverhampton foursome who seem to shout in tune and have a massive young following; **Middle Of The Road**, a folksy Glasgow group who took Europe by storm; and **The Sweet**, another foursome from West London with plenty of youth appeal.

In America, **The Osmonds**, five young white singers who gained fame on the Andy Williams TV shows, joined **The Jackson Five** and **David Cassidy/Partridge Family** in the weenybopper market, and on the heavier side the **Alice Cooper** group, full of weird showmanship and led by a male vocalist calling himself Alice Cooper, started to win a mass following.

The Beatles definitely stopped recording collectively and declared the group ended. But under the Apple banner, the members continued to make considerable contributions, such as **John Lennon's** *Imagine* and **Plastic Ono Band** LPs and a single, *Power To The People*; **Paul and Linda McCartney's** *Ram* LP and two big singles in *Uncle Albert/Admiral Halsey* and *Another Day*, as well as the start of their **Wings** group with its *Wild Life* album; **George Harrison's** *My Sweet Lord* and *All This Must Pass* LP (still popular from 1970), and **Ringo Starr's** *It Don't Come Easy* single.

Britain's new progressives won several Gold Discs: **Elton John** for three LPS — *Elton John*, *Friends*, and *Tumbleweed Connection*; **Emerson, Lake and Palmer** for *Tarkus* and another LP named after them; **Rod Stewart** for *Every Picture Tells A Story* LP and *Maggie May* single; and **Black Sabbath** for *Paranoid*, *Black Sabbath* and *Master of Reality*. **Derek and The Dominos** (**Eric Clapton's** new group) had *Layla* and **Cat Stevens** had two Golds for *Teaser And The Firecat*, and *Tea For The Tillerman*.

The young teen squad was well cared for by **The Osmonds** (*One Bad Apple*, *Yo Yo* and *Osmonds* LP) and 12-year-old **Donny Osmond** on his own (*Sweet And Innocent*, *Go Away Little Girl*) singles, and *Donny Osmond* LP); **The Jackson Five** (*Never Say Goodbye*, and *Mama Pearl*) and **Michael Jackson** (*Got To Be There*); **The Partridge Family** (*I'll Meet You Half Way*, *Doesn't Somebody Want To Be Wanted* singles, and *Up To Date*, *Sound Magazine* and *Christmas Card* LPs) and **David Cassidy**, star of the Partridge Family, with a single, *Cherish*.

In Britain, **The Sweet** won a Gold Disc with *Co-Co*; **Middle Of The Road** for *Chirpy Chirpy Cheep Cheep* and *Tweedle Dee Tweedle Dum*, and **The Slade** had big ones with *Get Down And Get With It* and *Coz I Luv You*. **The New Seekers**, after two years of trying, broke through with *Never Ending Song Of Love*, the **Fortunes** with *Freedom Come Freedom Go*, **East of Eden** with *Jig A Jig*, **Free** with *My Brother Jake*, and **Bay City Rollers** with *Keep On Dancing*. New singers were **Olivia Newton John**, from Australia (*If Not For You*, and *Banks Of Ohio*), **Hurricane Smith**, formerly the Pink Floyd's record producer (*Don't Let It Die*), **Tony Christie** (*I Did What I Did For Maria*) and **Labi Siffre** (*It Must Be Love*).

American girl vocalists were in much favour, with million-sellers from **Melanie** (*Brand New Key*, and *Candles In the Rain* LP), **Barbra Streisand** (with a progressive LP, *Stoney End*, and *Barbra Joan Streisand* LP), **Dionne Warwicke** (she added an 'e' to her surname and two more Gold LPs), **Judy Collins** (*Whales And Nightingales* LP), **Carole King** (*Tapestry* and *Carole King Music* LPs), the late **Janis Joplin** (*Pearl* LP), **Roberta Flack** (*Chapter Two* LP), **Joni Mitchell** (*Blue* LP), and **Aretha Franklin** (*. . . At The Fillmore West* LP).

Country and Western king **Charley Pride** had three more Gold LPs, **Lynn Anderson** had *Rose Garden*, a monster single and LP, **Merle Haggard and The Strangers** had *Fightin' Side Of Me*, **Ray Price** had *For The Good Times*, **Johnny Cash** had *The World Of . . .* LP, and **Jerry Reed** had a big single with *Amos Moses*.

Progressive music got heavier, with **The Rolling Stones** getting their own label named after them and bringing out their million-selling *Sticky Fingers* LP, and other Gold Disc LPs came from **The Who's** *Next*, **Santana**, **Chicago**, the late **Jimi Hendrix** (*The Cry Of Love*), three from **Three Dog Night**, two more from **Grand Funk Railroad**, and one each from **Guess Who**, **The Allman Brothers Band**,

Joan Baez sang protest songs and enjoyed great popularity

1
Blue Mink

2
Middle of the Road

Jethro Tull, Blood Sweat and Tears, Moody Blues (a big one with *Every Good Boy Deserves Favour*), Doors, James Gang, Mountain, and Ten Years After.

Vocal groups to win Golds were Crosby Stills Nash and Young (*Four Way Street*), splitting into David Crosby's *If I Could Only Remember My Name* LP, Graham Nash's *Songs For Beginners* LP, and Stephen Stills' *2* LP; the Fifth Dimension with two Gold LPs and The Carpenters with another.

Male vocalists were not so numerous in the Gold LP list — Tom Jones (*I Who Have Nothing*), Neil Diamond (*Taproot Manuscript*), Elvis Presley (*On Stage February 1970*, to mark his return to live performances after 13 years, at the Las Vegas International Hotel, and a Country LP), Andy Williams (*Love Story* and *Greatest Hits*, with *Home Loving Man* selling well in Britain), James Taylor (*Mud Slide Slim*), Engelbert Humperdinck (*Sweetheart*) and John Denver (*Poems, Prayers and Promises*). The two outstanding soundtrack albums were from films: "Love Story" and "Fiddler On The Roof".

Among the million-selling single songs of the year were *Just My Imagination* (Temptations), *Mercy Mercy Me* (Marvin Gaye), *I'm Still Waiting* (Diana Ross), *Groove Me* (King Floyd), *Gypsy Woman* (Brian Hyland), *Don't Pull Your Love* (Hamilton, Joe Franks & Reynolds), *Treat Her Like A Lady* (Cornelius Brothers and Sister Rose), *Rose Garden* (Lynn Anderson), *Precious Precious* (Jackie Moore), *Have You Ever Seen The Rain* (Creedence Clearwater Revival), *Don't Let The Green Grass Fool You* and *Don't Knock My Love* (Wilson Pickett), *She's A Lady* (Tom Jones), *Lovely Days*, and *How Can You Mend A Broken Heart* (Bee Gees), *For All We Know*, *Rainy Day And Monday*, and *Superstar* (Carpenters), *Battle Hymn Of Lt Calley* (Terry Nelson), *Put Your Hand In The Hand* (Ocean), *Proud Mary* (Ike and Tina Turner), *Bridge Over Troubled Waters*, and *Spanish Harlem* (Aretha Franklin), *Want Ads*, and *Stick Up* (Honey Cone), *Stay Awhile* (The Bells), *Indian Reservation* (The Raiders), *It's Too Late* (Carole King), *Take Me Home Country Roads* (John Denver), *Bring The Boys Home* (Freda Payne), *Help Me Make It Through The Night* (Sammi Smith), *You've Got A Friend* (James Taylor), *Ain't No Sunshine* (Bill Withers), *The Night They Drove Old Dixie Down* (Joan Baez), *Tired Of Being Alone* (Al Green), *Thin Line Between Love And Hate* (Persuaders), *Gypsies Tramps And Thieves* (Cher), *Family Affair* (Sly and The Family Stone), *An Old Fashioned Love Song* and *Joy To The World* (Three Dog Night), and *Clean Up Woman* (Betty Wright).

Popular hits in Britain during the year were *Hot Love* and *Get It On* by T Rex, featuring teen-rave Marc Bolan; *Rosetta* by organists Georgie Fame and Alan Price, who teamed up; *There Goes My Everything* by Elvis Presley, who revived the Humperdinck hit, and also had a three-tune single revival of his first rock hits, *Heartbreak Hotel, Hound Dog, Don't Be Cruel*, in the charts; *Remember Me* by Diana Ross; *Knock Three Times* by Dawn, featuring former rock singer Tony Orlando; *Brown Sugar* by The Rolling Stones; *Devil's Answer* by Atomic Rooster; *Resurrection Shuffle* by Ashton Gardiner and Dyke; *Lady Rose* by Mungo Jerry; *Ernie* by Benny Hill; *Witch Queen Of New Orleans* by Redbone; *Hey Girl Don't Bother Me* by The Tams; *Banner Man* by Blue Mink; *You Me And A Dog Named Boo* by Lobo; *I'm Gonna Run Away From You* by Tami Lynn, *Butterfly* by Frenchman Daniel Gerard; and *River Deep Mountain High* by the combined Supremes and Four Tops. Reggae had four big hits with Dave and Ansell Collin's *Double Barrel*, Bruce Ruffin's *Rain*, Bob and Marcia's *Pied Piper*, and The Greyhound's *Black And White*.

Three new names appeared in the British LP charts — Isaac Hayes with his "Shaft" film soundtrack of exciting jazz-rock music, Greek singer Nana Mouskouri with *Turn On The Sun* and *Over And Over*, and a wild band from Africa, Osibisa. Led Zeppelin II, Deep Purple *In Rock*, Simon and Garfunkel's *Bridge Over Troubled Waters*, and Andy Williams' *Greatest Hits* had stayed in the "New Musical Express" LP charts for more than a year!

In 1971, Peter, Paul and Mary broke up to work separately. Tom Fogerty left Creedence Clearwater Revival, who seemed to disappear from the charts, and British guitarist Jeremy Spencer quit the Fleetwood Mac group to join an American religious sect. It was revealed that three groups in the charts, Weathermen (*It's That Same Old Song*), Sakkarin (*Sugar Sugar*) and Piglets (*Johnny Reggae*), were all one person — Jonathan King, who had single hits in his own name! Mick Jagger got married in St Tropez to Bianca Macias and Reprise Records announced that *Sinatra And Company*, a double-album, would be the last new one Frank Sinatra would ever make, so it got into the charts very quickly. Louis Armstrong died at the age of 71 and was singing and playing his trumpet to the last. Jim Morrison, star vocalist of The Doors, died aged 28 in Paris.

1

3

2

4

6

1
Nana Mouskouri

2
Olivia Newton-John

3
The Sweet

4
Isaac Hayes

5
Emerson Lake and Palmer
(from left, Gregg Lake,
Keith Emerson and Carl
Palmer)

6
The Slade

1
Dave and Ansell Collins

2
John Denver

1

2

ELTON JOHN combines strong vocals with energetic piano playing on his hit recordings

DONNY OSMOND is the lead singer with the world-famous Osmonds pop singing group

1972

During this year more recording companies sprang up, which meant more releases, more competition and more artists than ever entering the American and British LP and single charts. The superstar badly needed by the industry didn't materialise, but some bright new talent came onto the scene, including **Don McLean**, a composer-singer who had sought fame since 1964; **Al Green**, 26, a rhythm-and-blues singer from Arkansas; **Donny Hathaway**, another smooth American singer; **Vicky Leandros**, an experienced Greek songstress who won the Eurovision Song Contest; **America**, a trio of young American musicians living in England; **Peter Skellern**, a youthful North of England composer-pianist-singer; **Lynsey de Paul**, a new personality vocalist, and **Roxy Music**, an energetic progressive music group. And not strictly new, but breaking through as a glamour performer was **David Bowie**.

Another dazzling arrival was **Gary Glitter**, the new name for a rather unsuccessful rock singer called Paul Raven, who rock'n'rolled his way to great fame in 1972, when the old styled rock and beat of the early '60s led to re-appearances in the charts of such oldies as **The Drifters'** *At The Club*, **B. Bumble and The Stingers'** *Nut Rocker*, and **Little Eva's** *Locomotion*, and a massive one-day event at Wembley Stadium, London, where some 80,000 packed the famous home of the English Cup Final football game to see such rock'n'roll giants as **Chuck Berry**, **Jerry Lee Lewis**, **Little Richard**, **Bo Diddley**, **Gary Glitter**, **Lord Sutch** and many more.

During the year the British Parliament had before it the Night Assemblies Bill, which, if it became law, could do away with all-night pop festivals. "New Musical Express" led a Kill The Bill campaign and won the day, when the Bill was thrown out. Several festivals could go on, most notably the big three-day event at Lincoln, featuring **Faces**, **Strawbs**, **Beach Boys**, **Rory Gallagher**, **Joe Cocker**, **Don McLean**, **Sha Na Na**, **Lindesfarne**, **Slade**, etc.

Elvis Presley had yet another good year, making a most successful appearance at Madison Square Gardens, New York, where he thought he could never do well, and won another Gold Disc for sales of the album recorded during his concert there. He also topped the American singles chart again with *Burning Love*, and had two other 1972 hits with *Until It's Time For You To Go* and *An American Trilogy*. **Stevie Wonder** completed nine years of hits at the age of 21, and **T. Rex** claimed to have sold 14 million discs in 12 months.

The weenyboppers protested so vehemently about the dropping of "The Partridge Family" by BBC TV that ITV started showing it almost immediately. The outrageous **Alice Cooper** came to London with its Cobra snake dance and hanging scene during its awesome act, and **Paul McCartney** took **Wings** on a European tour. **Gilbert O'Sullivan** and **Slade** sold-out everywhere on separate British tours.

The surprise success of the year was a million-selling single and LP of *Amazing Grace*, played by the **Royal Scots Dragoon Guards' Pipes, Drums and Orchestra**, which sold all over the world. And the **Vienna Philharmonic Orchestra** got into the British Charts with *Onedin Theme*, from BBC TV.

Among the world's best selling albums by British artists of 1972 were: **Faces** (*A Nod's As Good As A Wink*), **Traffic** (*Low Spark Of High-Heeled Boys*), **The Who** (*Meaty Beaty Big And Bouncy*), **Rolling Stones** (*Exile On Main Street*, *Hot Rocks 1964–71* and *Milestones*), **Elton John** (*Madman Across The Water* and *Honky Chateau*), **Humble Pie** (*Rockin' The Fillmore*, and *Smokin*), **Yes** (*Fragile*), **Tom Jones** (*. . . At Caesars Palace*), **Engelbert Humperdinck** (*Another Time Another Place*), **New Led Zeppelin** album, **Moody Blues** (*Days Of Future Past*, *Seventh Sojourn* — both in US LP chart Top Ten at same time), **Cat Stevens** (*Catch Bull At Four*), **Gilbert O'Sullivan** (*Himself*), **David Bowie** (*Ziggy Stardust*), **Rod Stewart** (*Never A Dull Moment*), **Hollies** (*Distant Light*), **Procol Harum** (*Live*), **Lindesfarne** (*Fog On The Tyne*), **The Jeff Beck** Group LP, **Jethro Tull** (*Thick As A Brick*), History of **Eric Clapton**, **Deep Purple** (*Machine Head*), **Jimi Hendrix** *in the West*, **Emerson Lake and Palmer** (*Pictures at an Exhibition*, and *Trilogy*), **Family** (*All in the Family*), **T. Rex** (*Electric Warrior* and *Bolan Boogie*), **Gary Glitter** (*Glitter*), and **Neil Reid** (*Neil Reid*), a 12-year-old boy singer.

The Anglo-American album of the year, and one of the best in 1972, was *The Concert For Bangla Desh*, which raised an incredible 243,418 dollars at Madison Square Gardens on August 1, 1971, organised by **George Harrison**, who played with **Bob Dylan**, **Eric Clapton**, **Billy Preston**, **Leon Russell**, **Klaus Voormann**, **Badfinger** and other singers and musicians. **Ravi Shankar**, Indian classical master of the sitar, also played on the concert, which was made into a three-album, boxed set and raised another fortune for the war refugees.

David Bowie assumed a glamour image and broke through in 1972

1
Lynsey de Paul

2
Neil Reid

3
Bill Withers

4
Gary Glitter

Americans with big-selling albums during 1972 were **Don McLean** (*American Pie*), **America** group LP, *Greatest Hits of:* **Blood Sweat and Tears**, **Bob Dylan** and **Simon and Garfunkel**; **John Denver** (*Aeries*), **Neil Diamond** (*Stones*, and *Moods*), **Alice Cooper** (*School's Out*, and *Killer*), **Joan Baez** (*Blessed Are*, and *Any Day Now*), **Leon Russell** (*. . . and Shelter People*, and *Carney*), **Charley Pride** *Sings Heart Songs*, **Harry Nilsson** (*Nilsson Schmilsson*), **Paul Simon** (first solo album), **Bread** (*Baby I'm A Want You*), **Allman Brothers Band** (*Eat A Peach*), **Cher**–*Cher-Cher*, **Robert Flack** (*First Take*, *Quiet Fire*, and *Young Gifted And Black*), **Al Green** (*Let's Stay Together*, and *You Ought To Be With Me*), comedians **Cheech and Chong** (*Cheech and Chong*, and *Big Bamboo*), **Santana** (*New Santana*, *Caravanserai*, and *Carlos Santana and Buddy Miles*), **Carole King** (*Rhymes and Reasons*), **Temptations** (*All Directions*), **Chuck Berry** (*London Session*) and **Three Dog Night** (*Seven Separate Fools*), **Bill Withers** (*Still Bill*), **Stephen Stills Manassas**, **Graham Nash** and **David Crosby** LP, **Neil Young** (*Harvest*), **Isaac Hayes** (*Black Moses*, and *"Shaft"* soundtrack), **Andy Williams** (*Theme from "The Godfather"*), **Jack Jones** (*Breadwinners*), **Aretha Franklin** (*Young Black And Beautiful*).

And for the weenyboppers there were these LPs – **Jackson Five's** *Greatest Hits*, **Jermaine** (*Jackson*), **David Cassidy's** *Cherish*, **The Partridge Family's** *Shopping Bag*, **The Osmonds'** *Home Made*, *Osmonds* and *Phase III*, and **Donny Osmond's** *Portrait Of . . .*, and *To You With Love*.

The songs that became big singles in 1972 included *American Pie* and *Vincent* (**Don McLean**), *Come What May* (**Vicky Leandros**), *I'd Like To Teach The World To Sing*, *Circles* and *Beg Steal Or Borrow* (**The New Seekers**), *Over And Over* (**Nana Mouskouri**), *Reflections On My Life* and *Radancer* (**Marmalade**), *Son Of My Father* (**Chicory Tip**), *The Lion Sleeps Tonight* (**Robert John**), *Got To Be There*, *Rockin' Robin*, *Too Late To Turn Back Now*, and *Ben* (**Michael Jackson**), *Sugar Daddy*, *Little Bitty Pretty One* (**Jackson Five**), *Hey Girl*, *Puppy Love*, *Too Young*, and *Why* (**Donny Osmond**), *Down The Lazy River* and *Crazy Horses* (**Osmonds**), *Long Haired Lover From Liverpool* (**Jimmy Osmond**, aged 9), *How Can I Be Sure* and *Could It Be Forever* (**David Cassidy**), *It's One Of Those Nights* and *Breaking Up Is Hard To Do* (**The Partridge Family**), *Hi Ho Silver Lining* (**Jeff Beck**), *Crocodile Rock* (**Elton John**), *Look Wot You Dun*, *Mama Weer All Crazee Now*, and *Gudbuy T'Jane* (**Slade**), *Rock'n'Roll Pt 1 and 2*, and *I Didn't Know I Loved You* (**Gary Glitter**), *Poppa Joe*, *Little Willy* and *Wig Wam Bam* (**Sweet**).

More big single tunes were *Without You* (**Nilsson** – five weeks at No. 1 in the British charts), *No Matter How I Try*, *Alone Again* (*Naturally*), and *Clair* (**Gilbert O'Sullivan**), *Give Ireland Back To The Irish* and *Mary Had A Little Lamb* (**Wings**), *Jeepster*, *Telegram Sam*, *Metal Guru*, and *Children Of The Revolution* (**T. Rex**), *One Monkey Don't Stop No Show* (**Honey Cones**), *Black Dog* (**Led Zeppelin**), *Floy Joy* (**Supremes**), *My World* (**Bee Gees**), *Mother And Child Reunion* and *Me and Julio Down By The School Yard* (**Paul Simon**), *I Gotcha* (**Joe Tex**), *Horse With No Name* (**America**), *First Time I Saw Your Face* (**Roberta Flack**), *Song Sung Blue* (**Neil Diamond**), *I Didn't Get To Sleep At All* (**Fifth Dimension**), *School's Out*, *Elected* (**Alice Cooper**), *Lean On Me* (**Bill Withers**), *Tumbling Dice*, *Happy* (**Rolling Stones**), *Nights In White Satin* and *Isn't Life Strange* (**Moody Blues**), *Don't Mess Around With Jim* (**Jim Croce**), *Daddy Don't You Walk So Fast* (**Wayne Newton**), *I Can See Clearly Now* (**Johnny Nash**), *My Ding-a-Ling* (**Chuck Berry**), *Power Of Love*, and *Drowning In A Sea Of Love* (**Joe Simon**), *Back Stabber* (**O'Jays**), *Kiss An Angel Good Morning* (**Charley Pride**), *You Are Everything*, *Betcha By Golly Wow* (**Stylistics**), *Black And White*, and *Never Been In Spain* (**Three Dog Night**), *Join Together* (**The Who**), *You're A Lady* (**Peter Skellern**), *Hallelujah Freedom* (**Junior Campbell**, ex-**Marmalade**), *Mouldy Old Dough* (**Lieutenant Pigeon**), *Sugar Me* (**Lynsey de Paul**), *Virginia Plain* (**Roxy Music**), *You Wear It Well* (**Rod Stewart**), *Popcorn* (**Hot Butter**), *Starman*, *John I'm Only Dancing*, and *Jean Genie* (**David Bowie**), *The Young New Mexican Puppeteer* (**Tom Jones**), *Back Off Bugaloo* (**Ringo Starr**), *Jesus* (**Cliff Richard**), *Meet Me On The Corner* and *Lady Eleanor* (**Lindesfarne**), *Say Don't You Mind* (**Colin Blunstone**), *Moon River* (**Greyhound**), *Mother Of Mine* (**Neil Reid**), *Have You Seen Her* (**Chi-Lites**), Theme from *"Shaft"* (**Isaac Hayes**), *Softly Whispering I Love You* (**Congregation**), *Soley Soley*, and *Sacramento* (**Middle of the Road**) and *Something Tells Me* (**Cilla Black**).

Tragedies of the year were the death of **Clyde McPhatter**, 41, founder of **The Drifters** and a solo artist, and the electrocution of lead guitarist **Les Harvey**, of **Stone The Crows**, by holding a 'live' microphone at Swansea.

1

2

3

1
Don McLean

2
Nilsson

3
America

1
The Osmonds, with little
Jimmy in front of Donny

2
Lindisfarne

3
Junior Campbell

4
Elton John

5
Roxy Music

3

4

5

1973

Most interesting news of the year until April was that Allen Klein, the New York businessman, did not want to manage the affairs of **John Lennon, George Harrison, Ringo Starr** or Apple Corporation any longer (they said it was mutual), the result being that **Paul McCartney** might re-join his former **Beatle** partners and more Lennon-McCartney songs would emerge, and **The Beatles** might record and perform together again.

The Strawbs, a popular British group who wrote songs about to-day, created much controversy (and got to No. 1) with *Part Of The Union*, the lyric saying in effect that the unions ran the country. British **Presley** fans were angry that neither BBC nor ITV would show Elvis' "Hawaiian Spectacular".

The original **Byrds** re-united for an LP, but **Paul Kossoff** quit **Free** for the second time and **Martha Reeves** left the **Vandellas** to become a solo artist. New outdoor venues in London to welcome pop during the summer were White City stadium on four Sundays and a 10-day event at Alexandra Palace, though two London Sundown rock theatres closed.

The "New Musical Express" Popularity Poll, based on readers' votes, resulted in wins for **Alice Cooper** and **Slade** (live groups), **Focus, Eric Clapton, Keith Emerson, Greg Lake, Carl Palmer, Paul McCartney, Elvis Presley, Maggie Bell, Rod Stewart** and **Roxy Music**, and **Slade** starred in the Poll Concert, which filled the Wembley Pool twice on a Sunday in March.

VAT, a new tax started in Britain on April 1, reduced the price of records fractionally by eliminating purchase tax.

Among the new discoveries to appear early in 1973 were **Little Jimmy Osmond**, aged 9, youngest of the famous **Osmonds**, who became the youngest ever performer to top the British charts, with *Long Haired Lover From Liverpool* (he followed with *Tweedle Dee*); **Focus**, a heavy group from Holland, who had three quick single hits, *Sylvia, Moving Wave* and *Hocus Pocus*; and **Thin Lizzy**, an Irish group, with *Whiskey In The Jar*.

Top LPs for the first four months of the year were **Carly Simons** *(No Secrets)*, **Jethro Tull** *(Living In the Past)*, **Seals and Crofts** *(Summer Breeze)*, **James Taylor** *(One Man Dog)*, **War** *(The World Is A Ghetto)*, **Curtis Mayfield** *(Super Fly)*, **Loggins and Messina** LP, **America** *(Homecoming)*, **London Symphony Orchestra, Chamber Choir, Pete Townshend, Roger Daltrey, Maggie Bell**, etc *(Tommy)*, **Elton John** *(Don't Shoot Me I'm Only The Pianist)*, **Deodato** *(Also Sprach Zarathustra, and Prelude)*, **Eric Weissberg** and **Steve Mandel** *(Duelling Banjos, from "Deliverance" soundtrack)*, **Traffic** *(Shout Out At Fantasy Factory)*, **John Denver** *(Rocky Mountain High)*, **Neil Diamond** *(Hot August Night)*, **Diana Ross** *("Lady Sings The Blues" soundtrack)*, **Stevie Wonder** *(Talking Book)*, **Joni Mitchell** *(For The Roses)*, **Marvin Gaye** *("Trouble Man" soundtrack)*, **Rolling Stones** *(More Hot Rocks)*, **Bette Midler** *(The Divine Miss M)*, **Helen Reddy** *(I Am A Woman)*, and **Elvis Presley** *(Elvis Aloha From Hawaii Via Satellite)*.

Slade *(Slayed, and Slade Alive)*, **Gilbert O'Sullivan** *(Back To Front)*, **Deep Purple** *(Made In Japan, and Who Do You Think We Are)*, **Cyril Ornadel** and **London Symphony Orchestra** *(Strauss Family)*, **Status Quo** *(Piledriver)*, **Focus** *(Focus 3)*, **Rick Wakeman** *(Six Wives Of Henry VIII)*, **Free** *(Heartbreaker)*, **Strawbs** *(Bursting At The Seams)*, **Little Jimmy Osmond** *(Killer Joe)*, **Beach Boys** *(Holland)*, **Max Bygraves** *(Sing Along With Max)*, **David Cassidy** *(Rock Me Baby)*, **Pink Floyd** *(Dark Side Of The Moon)*, **T. Rex** *(Tanx)*, **Led Zeppelin** *(Houses Of The Holy)*, **Roxy Music** *(For Your Pleasure)*, **Faces** *(Ooh La La)*, **Liza Minnelli** *(Liza with a Z)* and **Jack Jones** *(Together)*.

And the songs which made top singles during the first four months of 1973 included *You're So Vain* **(Carly Simon)**, *Me and Mrs Jones* **(Billy Paul)**, *Clair* **(Gilbert O'Sullivan)**, *It Never Rains In Southern California* **(Albert Hammond)**, *Crocodile Rock* **(Elton John)**, *Rockin' Pneumonia Boogie Woogie 'Flu* **(Johnny Rivers**, reviving a 1957 hit), *Superstition* **(Stevie Wonder)**, *Super Fly* **(Curtis Mayfield)**, *Your Mamma Don't Dance* **(Loggins and Messina)**, *I Wanna Be With You* **(Raspberry**, American mid-west group who featured Merseybeat), *Why Can't We Live Together* **(Timmy Thomas)**, *Last Song* **(Edward Bear**, a Canadian group), *Do You Wanna Dance* **(Bette Midler**, new song sensation), *Hi Hi Hi* **(Wings)**, *Don't Expect Me To Be Your Friend* **(Lobo)**, *Do It Again* **(Steely Dan)**, *Oh Babe What Would You Say* **(Hurricane Smith** topped US and UK charts with this one), *Could It Be I'm Falling In Love* **(Spinners)**, *Duelling Banjos* (from "Deliverance" soundtrack), *Killing Me Softly With His Song* **(Roberta Flack)**, *Daddy's Home* **(Jermaine Jack-**

Roy Wood of Wizzard, who topped the charts in 1973

son, another popular solo member of **The Jackson Five)**, *Love Train* **(O'Jays)**, *The Cover Of Rolling Stone* **(Dr Hook and The Medicine Show)**, *Danny's Song* **(Anne Murray)**, *I'm Just A Singer In A Rock'n'Roll Band* **(Moody Blues)**, *Ain't No Woman* **(Four Tops)**, *Neither One Of Us* **(Gladys Knight and The Pips)**, *Call Me* **(Al Green)**, *Aubrey* **(Bread)**, *Little Willy* **(Sweet)**, *Tie A Yellow Ribbon Round The Old Oak Tree* **(Dawn)**, *Sing* **(Carpenters)**, *The Cisco Kid* **(War)**, *The Night The Lights Went Out In Georgia* **(Vicky Lawrence)**, *Break Up To Make Up* **(Stylistics)**, *Stir It Up* **(Johnny Nash)**, *Pinball Wizard/See Me Feel Me* (**New Seekers** do **The Who's** songs), *Solid Gold Easy Action* **(T. Rex)**, *Happy Xmas* (War Is Over) **(John and Yoko and Plastic Ono Band)**, *Ball Park Incident* **(Wizzard, Roy Wood's** new group), *Wishing Well* **(Free)**, *Always On My Mind* **(Elvis Presley)**, *If You Don't Know Me By Now* **(Harold Melvin and Blue Notes)**, *Do You Wanna Touch Me*, and *Hello I'm Back Again* **(Gary Glitter)**, *Can't Keep It In* **(Cat Stevens)**, *Daniel* **(Elton John)**, *Blockbuster* **(Sweet)**, *Looking Through The Eyes Of Love* **(Partridge Family)**, *Take Me Girl I'm Ready* **(Jr. Walker and The All Stars)**, *Hello Hurray* **(Alice Cooper)**, *Doctor My Eyes* **(The Jackson Five)**, *Twelfth of Never* **(Donny Osmond)**, *Get Down* **(Gilbert O'Sullivan)**, *Power To All My Friends* **(Cliff Richard** came third in Eurovision Song Contest with this), *Cum On Feel The Noize* **(Slade)**, *Feel The Need In Me* **(Detroit Emeralds)**, *Heart of Stone* **(Kenny**, an Irish star), *I'm A Clown* **(David Cassidy)**, *Pyjamarama* **(Roxy Music)** and *Never Never Never* **(Shirley Bassey)**.

2

1

3

4

1
Loggins and Messina

2
Liza Minnelli

3
Thin Lizzy

4
Marc Bolan

5
Helen Reddy

6
Kenny

7
Simon Turner

1

2

3

4

5

6

7

And so, in May, 1973, I come to the end of the pop road from 1955 to the present day. What of the future? One thing is certain — a new superstar, individual or group, will appear. And quite soon. It is overdue. Who will be the next Elvis or Beatles? We don't know yet, but one will come. And then the record industry will soar to undreamt of sales and future potential.

Not that it is in any sort of slump at the present moment. Records sell in greater numbers every year. How long will we have records in their present form? For a few years yet, but gradually tapes in the form of casettes and 8-track cartridges, which we already have of course, will take over. They are more compact, more portable, lighter and improvements in them and their players are continually being made. 'In-car' entertainment will expand enormously and the time is not far distant when a stereo player will be standard in every new car, with every filling station selling tapes from slot-machine dispensers.

The visual (video) tape is on its way to the mass market, too. We will have a second TV screen beside our present one, on which we will be able to play pre-recorded tapes which will show us our recording stars as well as letting us hear them. On the same machine we will be able to record any TV programme for action-replay any time, whether we are there or not to see the original programme.

We are heading for a leisure age and listening to music will become an ever greater pastime. Every kind of musical taste will be catered for, from the weenyboppers (who usually have mums and dads listening to their music, too), to the way-out, hippy hard rock fans. New kinds of music will emerge, possibly from electronics. Pop music, too may move closer to classics. We have seen pioneer efforts in this by **The Procol Harum**, **Barclay James Harvest** group, **The Deep Purple**, **The Bee Gees** and **The Who's** "Tommy" pop opera, all of whom used symphony orchestras to supplement their group music.

Orchestral pop music, as conducted by **Mantovani**, **Burt Bacharach**, **Henry Mancini** and others will also endure the test of time and produce even better records in the future. And pop music cycles will demand that old styles, like rock'n'roll, will be revived and old records will become popular again, as we have seen recently.

Top stars will survive. **Elvis Presley**, now 38, is proof of how durable a versatile singer, properly managed as he has been by Colonel Tom Parker, can be. He shows no sign of losing his popularity, and neither does **Cliff Richard**, or **Tom Jones** or **Engelbert Humperdinck**. Recording companies are astute to keep signed, and happy, their big stars. **Bob Dylan**, for instance, was paid in advance the value of £2-million by Columbia Records for his next six, as yet uncomposed, albums! Songwriter-singers like **Gilbert O'Sullivan**, **Don McLean**, **Peter Skellern**, **Elton John**, **Marc Bolan**, **David Bowie**, **Pete Townshend** (of **The Who**), **Ray Davies** (of **The Kinks**) and many, many more have a lot more to offer us. And groups with the enthusiasm and daring to do something different will continue to pour excitement into pop music.

New artists will certainly come to the fore and some whom I have seen recently should progress in 1974, including an American coloured singer, **Maxine Weldon**, the sensitive actor-singer **Simon Turner**, the folky **Albert Hammond**, the Eastern-orientated **Mahavishnu Orchestra** — just four names which I think we will read more about in the future.

And who knows, within a year or two we may have **The Beatles** back together, performing as well as writing songs together again. Let's hope so, for the gifted combination of **John Lennon** and **Paul McCartney** is much needed.

The industry will continue to be well served by the Communicators, the disc jockeys and the music papers, who keep the ever-increasing pop music public informed on all the latest records.

Yes, the pop future looks very bright indeed. . . .

Elvis Presley, 38 in 1973, goes on forever